RACING ROGUES

The Scams, Scandals and Gambles of Horse Racing in Wales

Horse Racing in Wales Vol. 1

BRIAN LEE

St David's Press

Cardiff

Published in Wales by St. David's Press, an imprint of

Ashley Drake Publishing Ltd
PO Box 733
Cardiff
CF14 7ZY

www.st-davids-press.wales

First Impression – November 2016
Reprinted with revisions – February 2017

ISBN
Paperback – 978 1 902719 31 3
eBook – 978 1 902719 54 2

British Library Cataloguing-in-Publication Data.
A CIP catalogue for this book is available from the British Library.

Typeset by Replika Press Pvt Ltd, India
Printed by Akcent Media, Czech Republic

CONTENTS

PREFACE

The days when racecourse tipsters 'graced' our racecourses are long gone. But there will be some racegoers who will remember the likes of Ras Prince Monolulu, Gully Gully, Mike and The Captain – a smartly dressed man who was a regular at Chepstow Racecourse where he used to give out pencils and little notebooks as a way of drawing attention to himself.

Gully Gully always sported a teacher's mortar board and black gown and his cries of "Gully, Gully, Gully" would echo all around the course. His red sunburnt face could always be found at Chepstow, Newton Abbot and Devon & Exeter during the summer months.

The most famous of these tipsters was, of course, Ras Prince Monolulu. He used to wear a headband of dyed ostrich feathers and one of the lines he used to come out with was:

God made the bees
the bees made the honey
you have a bet and the
bookie takes your money

There were other sayings, but they wouldn't bear repeating here.

Mike's favourite trick to gather a crowd around him would be to throw down on the ground a huge wad of fivers held together by an elastic band and invite race goers to help themselves! Oddly enough, they never did.

A tipster of a different kind was the religious gentleman who would attend all the Chepstow race-meetings. With banner held high, he would stand for hour after hour by the numbers' board extolling race goers to mend their ways and save their souls.

However, unlike the "Can I mark your card, guv?" brigade, which used to hang around the car and coach parks, his advice came completely free of charge.

But just like these racecourse tipsters, who were out to relieve the racing public of their hard-earned cash, many of the characters you will be meeting in the ensuing pages were out to do exactly the same.

This book is dedicated to all those people, some now sadly no longer with us, who acted as my chauffeur, driving me to point-to-points and race-meetings all over the country.

FOREWORD

It's a great privilege to have been asked to write the foreword to this book which details so much of the diverse history of horse racing in Wales. There is no-one more qualified to have written it than Brian Lee who has been the *Western Mail*'s point-to-point correspondent for more than forty years and who is the author of more than twenty books.

The first time I met Brian was in 1975 I had published a facsimile of Tom Rees's *Racing Reminiscences* and he gave it some glorious reviews in a variety of journals and newspapers. As I got to know Brian better, I realised that if he hadn't been impressed with the book he would have said so. Indeed, because of his forthright opinions he has offended and pleased people in equal measures. He's been reported to the Jockey Club several times on the pretence of bringing hunt-racing in disrepute and on one occasion, some years ago, even getting himself banned from a point-to-point on the Welsh circuit because of his report of the day's events. Not that this deterred him as he turned up anyway to face his critics.

His Turf Talk column, which appears in the *Western Mail* every week, is the first thing I turn to on those mornings. He keeps Welsh racing alive with his punchy and informative stories and anyone remotely interested in horse racing in our part of the world will be familiar with it. It is the only one of its kind that deals with horse racing in Wales that is published in any journal.

When he approached me some 20 years ago - I was involved with a publishing company at the time - asking me if I was interested in publishing a little booklet on Cardiff's Ely Racecourse I readily agreed as

Robert King

I did later when he sent me a typescript for a book on Welsh steeplechase jockeys.

As kindred spirits we also share a passion for local history- Brian is the author of many books about his birthplace, Cardiff - and he was instrumental in finding me a publisher for my own books about Neath. He has always been supportive and has written many column inches about my own activities as an owner and rider and for the past 25 years a starter at my local point-to-point meeting. And when in the mid-eighties, my daughter and I had a great deal of success with a racing pony called Cennen Gambler which won on licensed racecourses in England he even got us air-time.

Brian has very kindly added some fascinating stories of the scandals, big gambles and the unusual and strange happenings that have occurred in racing albeit under the recognised rules or the unrecognised rules of the turf.

Robert King

ACKNOWLEDGEMENTS

I wish to thank all those who have helped me with this book. There are far too many to mention – you know who you are – but special thanks must go to my publisher, Ashley Drake, for giving me the opportunity to write this book, Brian Radford for writing the Introduction, Robert King for writing the Foreword, Tony Woolway at Media Wales and Alun Sedgmore of www.sportingprints.biz

Princess Anne talking to the author at the Golden Valley point-to-point in 2009, alongside her daughter Zara Phillips and the jockey Tom David

INTRODUCTION

BARRY BROGAN was a unique National Hunt jockey. When his controversial 15-year career ended in May 1977, he incredibly decided to put all his experiences in print as an autobiography, and invited me to write it for him.

Barry was unbelievably brave, fearless, astoundingly generous, addicted to betting and booze, and enjoyed nothing more than sneaking off with a trainer's wife or adult daughter—or both. He rode for the Queen Mother and drank for Ireland. He crashed cars in a haze as a hobby, competed in races after a pub-crawl, and gambled ferociously and badly. For ten seasons, he figured in the top five of Britain's elite band of National Hunt jockeys, and talked freely of the sport being awash with fixed races, huge bribes, gambling jockeys and crooked bookmakers. As a gambler, he once turned over £250,000 in six months, and lost a colossal £600,000 by the time common sense kicked in.

Barry lived with me and my family for three months while compiling his book, attending Gamblers' Anonymous on Tuesdays, and Alcoholics Anonymous on Thursdays. We will never forget those funny nights when he'd come back after an AA meeting weighed down by lager cans in a plastic bag, which he'd bought at the off-licence as a gift for the work I was doing. And he never touched a drop. It was as though he also bought them to test his abstinence. Barry was the proverbial 'likeable rogue'. Charming, inoffensive, polite, amusing, and never forgetting his bouquet of flowers every Friday for my wife as a 'thank you' for all the meals she cooked for him. Yet behind this smiling, plausible facade was a sharp, mischievous mind that set up all sorts of devious challenges that inevitably ended with a three-month spell in an open prison for stealing £2,000 from a bookmaker's car and losing the lot on four races in a betting shop across the road. Barry delighted in telling me how he volunteered to clean the prison chapel—and

Brian Radford

arranged for his friends to visit and drop cigarettes in the waste bins, which he rapidly emptied when everyone had left.

What must never be forgotten about Barry Brogan was his courage and skill as a jockey. He rode more than 400 winners, including illustrious victories at the Cheltenham Festival, Aintree, Ascot, and for royalty. Many times, he vanished overnight, boldly returning two to three weeks later claiming he'd been laid low by a serious stomach complaint, when in truth he'd been back in Ireland being dried out. But for these constant alcoholic interruptions, Brogan could well have been a champion. As it was, he was Northern champion five times. Before we sat down to write his book, he said to me... "This shall be the truth, the whole truth, and nothing but the truth." What he produced was dynamic and explosive. Nothing was left out. He insisted on the good, the bad, and the ugly. And because of his honesty and frankness, it was a pleasure to work with him.

Brogan's link with South Wales was inevitably dramatic and mysterious. Nothing he ever did was normal and predictable. He bought a horse in Ireland called Mount Shasta on behalf of permit-holder John Williams, who was based at Dinas Powis near Cardiff. Aware of the horse's true ability, Brogan followed it to Wales where he worked a 14-hour day carefully bringing it to its peak for a massive coup. He fed it, rode it at exercise, and drove it to the races. As part of the master plan, Mount Shasta ran four times before the big day. It was never less than 33-1 in the betting, and never finished better than ninth. The coup was plotted for Exeter racecourse on a quiet Monday when punters were still recovering from a busy weekend. There was no 33-1 available this time. Mount Shasta was ferociously backed to even-money favourite in a terrible selling race. Vast sums were bet in London, Birmingham, Coventry and Leicester. But the coup went horrendously wrong when a bridle pin snapped and the horse ran out in thick mist at the far end of the track with less than half the race completed. Jockey Club investigators were quickly on the scene, and the bridle was taken away and forensically examined by racing's security boffins. To this day it remains a frustrating mystery, as nothing ever emerged to confirm that it was a dreadfully unfortunate accident or whether someone wilfully tampered with the bridle before the race to wreck the coup.

As for Brogan, he insisted that he didn't bet the horse, and that it was the first time a bridle had snapped with him, and that the only explanation could be that the horse had caused it by pulling hard.

When we parted, with the manuscript complete, and his gambling and alcoholism totally conquered, he shook my hand, and said proudly "Thanks... The fugitive has finally stopped running..."

Many people genuinely believe that horse-racing's popularity has been sustained through its astounding ability to stumble from scams to corruptions, bent jockeys to crooked bookies, and a mass of ingenious strokes to keep punters perversely transfixed.

Flat jockey Jimmy Walsh, a legendary leg-puller, attempted the most audacious ruse to win a hurdle race in dense fog at Catterick. As he cantered to the start on a 100-1 no-hoper, a thick mist fell like a proverbial grey blanket right across the track. Visibility was barely 30 yards when the 23 runners shuffled into line, with the anxious starter bawling to the jockeys "Triers in front, the others behind." Just four moved forward. The fog was so thick that the runners were merely a cluster of ghostly shapes in the distance, and for most of the race could not be seen at all. Walsh quickly realised that no-one would know whether he'd raced the two miles or not, so he pulled his horse up and patiently waited for the other 22 to race around the track before joining in again, fresh and relaxed, as he heard them approaching. He streaked to the front in a two-furlong dash to the line but, alas, his horse was so bad that they were quickly overtaken and could finish no better than fifth!

Another classic con was carried out by a young, inventive Newmarket trainer who, on finding that he had a high-class sprinter, decided to run it in a low-class selling race at Warwick even though he knew that substantial bids would be made at the ensuing auction for his guaranteed winner. So he crucially needed to come up with a reason to convince any potential purchaser that this horse should not be bought at any price. And he did, quite brilliantly. It was arranged that the stable lad who would lead the horse to the winner's enclosure, should carry a syringe filled with pig's blood hidden under his jacket, and would produce it quickly, and squirt the blood over the jockey's silks and around the horse's nose. This slick ruse made it seem that the horse had burst a blood vessel, so there was not a single bid for it. Though the trick was used only once, punters and bookmakers always feared the horse would burst a blood vessel again, so its odds remained attractive. It won four times in all, landing gamble after gamble, and was always led away without a bid being offered. The stroke was never suspected, and it helped the trainer to assemble a large and prosperous stable.

For a trainer there is nothing more frustrating than having a horse with enormous ability but refuses to produce it on the racecourse. Canny Harry ended up with an exceptionally talented four-year-old who landed handicap races at York and Doncaster before it became totally unreliable at the start, often refusing to go off with the rest or, at best, giving them a 20-length lead. It was a sprinter with electrifying speed. And that's exactly what Harry decided it desperately needed—a few electric shocks! So he called on his local farmer and borrowed a section of fence powered by a six-volt battery that was used to keep cattle in a field. He immediately took the fence to the gallops where his jockey was lining the horse up, and slowly walked behind it, gently ticked its backside, and it flew...

Having solved the problem, Harry promptly prepared for a mammoth coup in a big race at Ayr, where only he, the jockey, and the horse's owner knew there would be no hanging around at the start. With punters and bookies putting no trust in the horse, its odds were a tremendous 20-1 when Harry left his position in the stands with just five minutes to the 'off' and hit the bookies so hard that it plunged to 5-1 favourite. Tension mounted around the course. Would the horse start? Would it whip round? Not this time. Fearing his bottom would be tickled, it leapt to the front, stayed there all the way, and won by a length and a half. Job done, gamble landed. Farmer got his fence back. Ingenious.

Which brings me to a masterful stroke repeatedly perpetrated by what I considered to be the shrewdest trainer in Britain during his 30 years in the business. His lucrative brainwave initially involved his charming wife, who proved to be highly skilled with needle and thread.

'Brush boots' are commonly fitted to protect the shins of horses in jump races. They are generally made of leather and strapped around the horse's legs. Well, this particular trainer decided to manufacture his own – using his wife's talents, of course – cleverly sewing small pockets behind the leather, in which up to 5lb of lead could be hidden. When he wished to slow a horse, he would slip the lead into the secret pockets on both front legs, and it would race carrying 10lb in overweight. No-one suspected this amazing scam, least of all the handicappers! This inevitably meant that handicappers would lower the weight they asked his horses to carry, and when they came down to a mark where they could effectively fall, get up, and enjoy a bag of oats, he took the lead from the pockets, and they romped home to land enormous bets. Michael 'X' was a truly brilliant Northern trainer who specialised in preparing bold, front-running steeplechasers to plunder major prizes.

On one occasion he sent a novice raider to Ascot for its first run of the season to challenge three previous winners in a six-horse race. Even though there was no known information on the horse's fitness or ability, someone somewhere clearly knew the facts as it was bet down to 3-1 favourite in a stampede before the 'off'.
Backers calmly relaxed all through the race, as the horse jumped superbly and led from start to finish, strolling home with two lengths to spare.

A few days later, someone high up in the winning stable came and sat next to me at Chepstow races. After complimenting him on their resounding Ascot success, I asked him when the horse would run again. A minor race at Catterick had been chosen for it, he said, "but it won't win!" Shocked and baffled, I snapped back: "For heaven's sake why not? Are you seriously saying that your easy Ascot winner won't follow up at little Catterick?" "Yes, that's right" he replied, nodding furiously to back up his extraordinary prediction. I stressed that the horse was bound to start favourite with punters piling their money on after seeing it win so easily at Ascot. He smiled and whispered, "Yes, but Ascot is a right-handed course, Catterick is left-handed, and this horse can't go left-handed. He'll jump badly to the right and lose around six to eight lengths at every fence. He'll be lucky to finish in the first three."

Catterick's unsuspecting punters bet it favourite and then glowered in disbelief as it jumped violently right at every fence before trailing in third, beaten 25 lengths.

Let that be a warning... It's the perfect example to confirm racing's most famous and accurate cliché 'There's no such thing as a certainty!'

When Brian Lee asked me to provide "as many words as you like" as an introduction to his book on Welsh racing scandals, it gave me this long overdue opportunity to extend a big 'thank you' to him for all the excellent reporting he did for me when I was the *Western Mail*'s racing editor. Brian concentrated on the Welsh point-to-point circuit, and through his enormous passion and dedication to detail he has become a walking encyclopedia on this highly important part of the racing world. I salute his success, and sincerely hope, and believe, this special book will be one to enjoy and retain as a true record of fascinating drama and mystery.

Brian Radford

1
THE RINGERS

1.1 THE SILVER BADGE AND SHINING MORE CONSPIRACY CASE

A report in the *Western Mail* dated October 22 1920 read: "The Stewards of the National Hunt Committee have disqualifed Jazz the winner of the Cottrill Novices Hurdle at Cardiff on Easter Monday and also disqualified Silver Badge which was in reality Shining More, winner of the Malvern Selling Race at the December Cheltenham Meeting."

Let us go back to that December 29, 1919 Cheltenham meeting to find out what that report was really all about. It was a fine day and crowds were flocking to the spiritual home of steeplechasing by car, bus and train to witness the riding skills of the famed Welsh jockey Jack Anthony who landed a brilliant hat-trick over the Prestbury Park course with Wavylace, Tally-Ho and Garryvoe.

The First World War over, people were beginning to enjoy themselves again and most of the large crowd were, understandably, still in good spirits after the Christmas holiday. The third race on the card was the Malvern Selling Hurdle run over two miles with prize money of 100 sovereigns. There were only six runners and the locally trained Governor Wood was made a 6/4 odds-on favourite. The Gnat was second best at 4-1, Tom Berney a 7-1 chance with the three remaining runners – Silver Badge, Mount Felix and Vaulx – all on offer at 10-1 or over.

It is worth mentioning that the last named was ridden by Lester Piggott's father Keith, who incidentally finished down the field, but went on the win the 1925 Welsh Grand National at Cardiff.

One of the runners on the racecard, which was trained privately by Samuel Berg, of Epsom, was described as "Silver Badge, a bay mare (pedigree unknown) purchased at Army Sale, Bristol, March 18, 1919." Shortly before the race, Cyril Lawley, aged 43, a motor-engineer of Wentworth Mansions, Hampstead, and the apparent owner of Silver Badge, had approached Tom Hulme, a well-known jockey, and asked him to ride Silver Badge telling him it was a good jumper. He offered him £50 to ride it and after agreeing to take the mount Hulme asked Lawley to get the mare saddled. Lawley did not seem to understand and it was left to his companion Peter Christian Barrie, a 32 year-old racehorse owner and amateur rider, to saddle up

Silver Badge. It came as a great shock to those who had backed the odds-on favourite, and indeed to most of the other punters, when the said Army remount, confidently ridden by Hulme won, easing up by six lengths from The Gnat with Governor Wood a further three lengths back in third place.

Very little interest had been shown in Silver Badge before the race. This was not really surprising as the mare had been almost covered with rugs. But, the race over, it did not take long for someone to smell a rat, as can be seen by this report which appeared in the *Western Mail* the next day: "The Malvern Selling Hurdle went to Silver Badge who, though starting without a quotation, was so much liked when she entered the sale ring that the bids went up to 510 guineas before the hammer fell." Then, in somewhat guarded terms, the report went on to say: "Silver Badge, as a matter of fact, might be a valuable mare, for no-one knows who she is or what she is. She may have won hurdle races and steeplechases innumerable under another name for anything anyone knows to the contrary, she being one of the animals who have left their identity completely behind them in France."

Seven months later, in July 1920, at Bow Street (London) Police Court, a turf conspiracy case began that was to shock the racing world. Before Graham Campbell K.C. were Norman Weisze, aged 40, London's biggest pearl merchant, who resided at Hailsham Road, Kensington, and Cyril Lawley. Both were charged with conspiracy along with Barrie, in that they tried to obtain money by fraud at Cheltenham Races by running the more than useful mare Shining More in the name of Silver Badge when in fact the latter horse never existed. To complicate matters, Barrie and a bloodstock dealer and trainer called Walter Hopkins, aged 42, of Ashstead, Surrey, had been previously charged with conspiring to obtain money from Messrs Weatherbys in connection with the alleged substitution of the three-year-old Jazz for the two-year-old Coat Of Mail at Stockton in the October of 1919.

However, in the Silver Badge/Shining More case, it was revealed that Weatherbys had received a letter from 86 Belsize Lane, Hampstead, which had been signed by a Cyril S Lawley, Lieut. R E(retired) describing how he had purchased a mare at some Army Sales yard held in Bristol. He told, in his letter, that he had been unable to trace the mare's pedigree, but he wished to enter her for the Malvern Selling Hurdle in the name of Silver Badge. A few days later, Weatherbys having replied to the letter, Lawley called on them and gave them the information identifying the mare he had described as aged, brown in colour, and of unknown pedigree. The court heard how on the morning of the race ,the Clerk of the Course received a telegram from Lawley, giving the racing colours in which Silver Badge would be running and declaring her weight as 11st 13lb. They also heard how jockey Tom Hulme was engaged at the last minute, for a fee of £50 and how Barrie, having been seen giving him his riding instructions before the start, took his place in the stands to watch the mare win very easily indeed. In accordance with the conditions of the race, the winner was put up for auction. This was where Norman Weisze, the actual owner of Shining More, became involved.

There was some brisk bidding and Weisze, as Mr Norman, had to go to 510 guineas to buy back the mare. No doubt it was the fact that Weisze, who had put up the money to organise the coup, was prepared to go to 510 guineas, a considerable sum then, to buy the mare back that started tongues wagging and enquiries to be made. The cause of the perpetrators was not helped when it was discovered that the owner's address was entered as Downs, Hurst, Epsom, instead of Belsize Lane, Hampstead. Enquiries at Epsom soon revealed the fact that a day or two before the race the mare Shining More had left Samuel Berg's Epsom stables and was sent to Waterloo. Later the horse was traced to Cheltenham and eventually back to London. When Shining More was brought up from Epsom stables she was subjected to some treatment which made her colour very dark. Also, a white blaze on her forehead, along with a white patch on her hind fetlock, were completely obliterated.

Stable lad Alexander MacFarlane, employed by Barrie at Downs House, Epsom, told the court that Barrie had one or two good horses in the yard including Shining More, which he described as a very good mare. In fact, Shining More had actually won at Cheltenham a month before she scored over the same course under her false name, Silver Badge. MacFarlane told how, on Barrie's instructions, he had taken Shining More from Epsom to Hampstead and went to fetch her back after the race.

When Berg was questioned by the police at Epsom Police Station he said: "Treat me kindly. I shall give you no trouble. I was going to give myself up. Whatever I have done I have been the dupe of others. I know nothing about Jazz or Coat Of Mail. I trained Shining More. I got permission from the Jockey Club to train for Mrs Barrie. I know that Shining More went and ran at Cheltenham and when it came back to my yard I could not believe it was the same horse. It had been coloured over and it had been well pulled."

As it happened, they had made such a good job of disguising Shining More that pints of petrol and other cleaners had to be used to get the mare back to her natural colour. During the trial, Cheltenham Course bookmaker Louis Burnett told how Weisze had placed £600 on Silver Badge. Several different off-course bookmakers gave evidence that they had accepted from

Weisze one bet of £100 by telephone half-an-hour or so before the race, another of £500 and a third of £25. But how much was wagered off the course in telegrams, no-one will ever know.

For his part in the conspiracy, Weisze, who had left Hungary in 1890 to live in England, was sentenced to 15 months jail and after council had contended that the verdict was a grave miscarriage of justice, leave to appeal was granted.

Lawley was fined just £100, the judge taking an extremely lenient view, while Barrie, the only one to plead guilty to all the charges against him, was sentenced to three years penal servitude. Justice Greer said in sentencing the former Australian soldier, who had been wounded at Gallipoli, that he was: "One of the prime movers in a series of racing frauds." Berg, who was found guilty in this particular case, was sentenced to nine months for his part in another racing fraud involving the running of a three-year-old in a two-year-old race.

However, like the Jazz and Coat Of Mail affair that's another story altogether.

1.2 THE RINGER SCANDAL THAT SHOCKED THE RACING WORLD

On August Bank Holiday Monday 1978, bookmakers at Newton Abbot Racecourse were stunned when a horse down on the racecard as In The Money, which had been backed from 33-1 to 8-1 before the bookmakers refused to take any more bets on it, stormed home a 20 lengths winner of the Hatherleigh Selling Hurdle race. The horse, which was supposed to have been racing for the first time in three years, was ridden by Welsh jockey John Williams, one of a handful of jockeys who can claim to have ridden in the Derby and the Grand National.

In The Money's trainer, Crickhowell's John Bowles, a former amateur rider of note, who was saddling his first winner as a trainer, had to go to 1,100 guineas to retain the horse at auction following the race which had netted him £525 in prize money. One of the bookmakers on the racecourse that day was Cardiff's George Parsons, secretary of the Welsh Bookmakers Association. He was to tell the press: "With

John Bowles

20 bookmakers at the course there was a minimum of £15,000 to £20,000 paid out to backers. That was without reckoning what could have been won off the course and on the Tote."

With bets placed at bookmaking shops throughout the country, the betting coup was later thought to have netted around £65,000, quite a considerable sum in 1978. With this amount of money involved and the amazing improvement in form by the horse in question it was little wonder that racecourse security officers on behalf of the Jockey Club began to make some enquires. After all, In The Money, later to be described as "A pigeon-toed, broken down hack" had ran half-a-dozen or so times in the past and had failed to complete the course on each occasion!

Calling at Bowles's training yard, so that they could compare the identity marks on In The Money's official passport documents, the Jockey Club officials learned that the

John Williams

horse had been slaughtered at a Bristol abattoir the morning after the race. Bowles told them: "In The Money went lame and I did not wish to see the old boy suffer." However, following a tip-off received by former National Hunt jockey Taffy Salaman, who had been associated with Bowles but who

was then training at Lambourn, police later visited Bowles and asked him about another horse called Cobbler's March, a more than useful sort, and a winner of six races. Bowles admitted that he once had the horse in his yard.

He claimed that he had bought the horse for a local girl, Becky Beaumont, to ride in point-to-points adding that he didn't tell his wife as she might have thought that they were having an affair. He also said that Cobbler's March had died a few months before adding: "The horse never got fit for racing. It died in May. We gave

Taffy Salaman

John Bowles

proof to the Jockey Club and they accepted my explanation."

Miss Beaumont, then in her 20s, who lived near Abergavenny not far from Bowles's yard confirmed Bowles's story: "We don't have a relationship. He bought the horse for me only as a point-to-pointer."

However, by an amazing coincidence, a former owner of Cobbler's March, a racecourse photographer called Colin Wallace, who was on duty at Newton Abbot that day, had in the past taken pictures of both In The Money and Cobbler's March and still had them in his possession. It was mainly on photographic evidence that in 1980 after a two week trial at Exeter Crown Court, Bowles was given an 18 month suspended sentenced and fined £1,500 after being convicted on two counts of deception. Throughout the trial and afterwards, Bowles insisted that it was In The Money and not Cobbler's March that had won the Newton Abbot race.

The Jockey Club though had no doubts and declared him a disqualified person until the year 2000, one of the severest sentences to be handed out by the Jockey Club in the history of the turf. However, Bowles continually defied the Jockey Club ban and had the cheek to turn up at Newton Abbot in August 1986 where he was escorted from the racecourse by security staff. He was also a regular visitor to point-to-points and eight years after being warned off was fined £500 after attending various point-to-points and Cheltenham Racecourse.

In 1989 he failed in an appeal court bid to clear his name, claiming fresh evidence. The judges, headed by Lord Lane the Lord Chief Justice, refused to hear evidence from a former stable lad and apprentice jockey Jeffrey Kear who claimed that he had lied when he gave evidence for the Crown at Bowles's trial. That same year Bowles's son Lee was fined £50 by the Jockey Club. His horse Katesville, winner of the men's open at the Tredegar Farmers at Llantarnam in May was not qualified to be entered or start in the race as its parentage was not as previously recorded in the General Stud Book. The disciplinary committee of the Jockey Club considered the evidence, including a written request from Mr Bowles that the committee deal with the evidence in his absence, and found him to be in breach of Jockey Club regulations. His father was also fined £1,000 after the same disciplinary committee ruled that he had been in breach of Jockey Club regulations by attending the Pentyrch point-to-point on April 22 while a disqualified person. In a statement to the Jockey Club, Bowles had admitted that he had attended the meeting.

Under the heading 'BANNED BOWLES GOES TO IRELAND', an exclusive report of mine appeared in *The Sporting Life* on June 4, 1990 which read: 'WARNED-OFF Welsh trainer John Bowles is leaving Crickhowell to live in Ireland. Bowles, 46, failed in an Appeal Court bid last year to clear his name for his part in a ringer scandal ten years ago. He said: "I am going to live in a little place called Dooleek." The former amateur rider added: "I am fed up with not being able to share in my son Lee's success and not being able to take part in the sport I love."

This season Lee Bowles has trained 11 point-to-point winners and on Saturday he received the Belstaff Point-To-Point Owners Association's young horse award, which he won with The Screamin Demon, at a special luncheon presentation at Stratford racecourse. He is also the owner-trainer of Wales's leading point-to-pointer Katesville.

Last season John Bowles, who was fined £500 for attending Cheltemham and point-to-points the previous year defied a Jockey Club ban by attending point-to-point meetings. But this season he decided to stay away so, as his son put it, that he, "would not be hounded." Bowles lost his trainers' licence in 1980 and was declared a disqualified person for 20 years after a jury found that in 1978 he had switched his ten-year-old maiden In The Money with Cobbler's March, a winner of six races, in a selling hurdle at Newton Abbot's Bank Holiday Monday meeting. Bowles said that he would only return home from time to time to take care of his business interests.'

1.3 GOMER CHARLES AND THE FASCINATING FRANCASAL AFFAIR

Walking home from the *Western Mail* offices in Cardiff, in the early hours of the morning of December 12 1966, after finishing my night shift, I saw two policemen standing outside number 22 Park Place which was the residence of Mr Gomer Charles.

I was soon to learn that Mr Charles, who has been aptly described as "a jolly looking, double chinned Welsh bookmaker", had, around seven hours earlier, been killed. Two men had rung his doorbell and when he

Gomer Charles

had opened the door, one of them threw pepper in his face and the other shot him in the chest.

Twelve years earlier Mr Charles, then aged 46, had found himself in the dock of the Old Bailey along with Henry George Kateley, 42, a Maidenhead bookmaker, Victor Robert Colquhoun Dill, 56, a Chelsea dealer, William Morris Williams, 47, a builder's assistant from Kentish Town and William Rook, 57, an engineer from Buckinghamshire. They had all pleaded not guilty to conspiring to cheat and defraud Bath Racecourse Company by falsely representing that a horse running in the two o'clock race at Bath on July 18,1953, in the name of Francasal, was in fact, Santa Amaro; and conspiring to win money by false pretences.

Had they not employed a Rhondda Valley scrap metal dealer called Leonard Phillips to scale a telegraph pole and cut through the 'blower' line which linked the racecourse to the outside world they might well have got away with it.

Mr Phillips, when he was charged with "unlawfully and maliciously cutting a cable, being part of a certain electric telegraph belonging to Her Majesty's Postmaster General, contrary to Section 37 of the Malicious Damage Act,1861," told the police, "A fellow I know as Bill came to see me. He offered me 35 nicker (pounds) to do the job... I am only a small end in the big wheel I don't know the big shots." Phillips went to jail for three months refusing to name his accomplice who was said to have actually cut the wire while Phillips held the ladder.

The coup had been planned some months earlier with the setting up of betting contacts throughout the land. Firstly, accounts were opened up with other bookmakers so that those involved could place bets on the horse that would win them a fortune. Then, to land a coup of this magnitude, two horses that looked alike were to be bought very discreetly. One of the perpetrators of the scam, Morris Williams, took a trip across the Channel to France where he bought two two-year-old bay colts. He paid £2,000 for Santa Amaro and £820 for Franscasal, whose form was inferior to that of Santa Amaro.

Writing about this scam, Brian Radford writes: "With Santa Amaro in their possession, the gang wasted no time in testing his ability. A private trial was arranged for twenty-five pounds at Worcester racecourse and Santa Amaro was pitted against two other sprinters in a six furlong gallop at 8.30 in the morning while the city was still waking up. Santa Amaro won impressively, confirming that he was a good horse and perfect for the job. The trial had been arranged by Gomer Charles and unbeknown to the

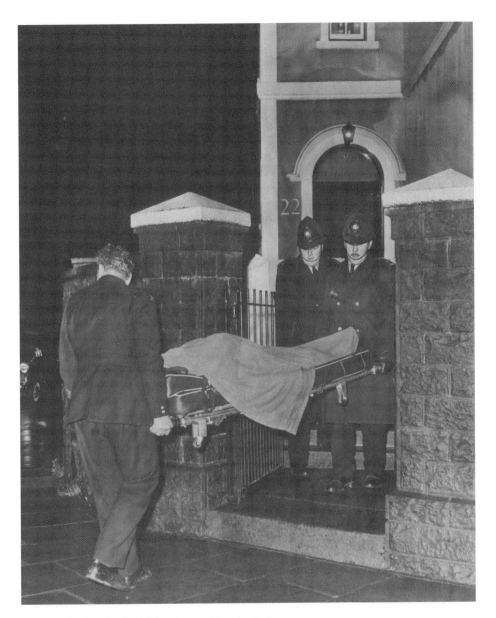

Gomer Charles' body being removed by the Police

jockeys who took part in it, Santa Amaro had carried 21lb of lead and had still finished two lengths ahead of the useful Della's Choice. To make sure no one got to hear of his ability, Santa Amaro was immediately sent back to France, and arrangements were made for him to remain there until close to the big day."

Benny Jacobs (right) with boxing critic Dave Phillips

On the day of the race, July 16, 1953, Santa Amaro – down on the race card as Francasal – and who had been delivered to the unsuspecting Percy Bailey's Epsom yard just three days earlier, was a 20-1 shot in *The Sporting Life*'s betting forecast. However, on the course, Francasal opened up a 6-1 chance but went out in the betting and was returned at 10-1. Commission agents all over the country took thousands of pounds in telephone bets on the little horse with none of the money getting back to the track owing to the blower service having been put out of operation.

In the parade ring before the race, the horse's jockey William Gilchrist was instructed by Bailey to hold the horse up and not to make his move until close to home. However, Francasal was much faster than any of the horses in the race and soon pulled himself in front and went on to win easily by a length and a half.

A police dog and his handler set out from the house

Charles was later to tell the court that he had accepted a bet of £2,500 on the horse. He said he was in his office on that day between noon and 1pm and Kateley, one of the accused, had asked him if he could put £2,500 on Francasal. Charles said he accepted the bet and laid it off. He had not bet on the horse himself and in addition, he said he had accepted a bet of £25 from a client in Merthyr which he did not lay off. When asked why he did not give full information concerning dealings with his clients he said: "I did not want to be called a squealer."

The size of the conspiracy was huge and it is estimated that, the modern equivalent of the bets placed by Gomer Charles and Robert Colquhoun Dill would be well in excess of £100,000.

The gang had given instructions that Francasal was to be bought back at any price in the auction following the race, for obvious reasons, and by the time he had been knocked down to them for 780 guineas, rumours of skulduggery were already in the air. Britain's biggest bookmaker, William Hill, faced a huge payout and was the first to ask the National Sporting League to investigate the matter. The Jockey Club wasted no time and held a meeting, chaired by the Duke of Norfolk. Following this, Scotland Yard Chief Superintendent Reginald Spooner was soon on the case.

The Grand Stand, Bath.
(Instantaneous Photograph by Our Special Artist.)

The old grandstand at Bath Races

Bridget Smit, who was a telephonist at the Cardiff telephone exchange at that time said, "My memory is of being summoned to the office by the chief supervisor and being told that I would have to give evidence at the Old Bailey because a call that I had connected was crucial in the evidence against Gomer Charles."

"Before subscriber trunk dialing – we knew it as S.T.D. but this now has a different connotation – each call connected via an operator had a written ticket showing exchange to and from, connecting time and duration. This was for charging the subscriber. I was 17 at the time and had never visited London. I was accompanied by a senior female employee and was told to dress smartly and wear a hat."

"On arrival at the Old Bailey we were met by Superintendent Spooner of the Yard. After a short briefing, we were shown into court number one. Actually my evidence only consisted of swearing that the ticket with the details had been written out by me at the time of the call. Even so, I was terribly nervous and when I had to walk across to the witness box in this

General scene Bath Races

famous criminal court I remember Gomer Charles looking at me and in my innocence thinking that he would come after me when he was released."

The trial itself was also a controversial affair, as after 28 days of evidence, the jury of ten men and two women retired twice and on both occasions failed to reach a verdict. At this point Judge Sellers ordered an immediate retrial and a new jury was sworn in with a new judge, Mr Justice Byrne. After a further four weeks the new jury had no difficulty in coming to a decision. After Justice Byrne's nine-hour summation, they reached their verdict after a further four hours of deliberation and convicted four of the five men.

All the defendants except Rook had been found guilty. Kateley was sentenced to prison for three years, Charles and Williams both got two years and Dill nine months.

The irony of the escapade was that had the gang run Santa Amaro in its own name, they would probably have cleaned up anyway and everyone would have been congratulating them on landing a perfectly legal betting coup.

A footnote to this case is the question as to other possible co-conspirators. A friend of mine called Reg Condon told me that Benny Jacobs, a well-known Cardiff boxing promoter and bookmaker had asked him to place a large bet on the horse for him. Reg, who also bet the horse for himself, was interviewed by the police afterwards and managed to convince them that he fancied the horse and that the bet he had on it was nothing unusual for him.

Cardiff-born Benny Jacobs has been described by Wynford Jones, one of Britain's longest serving boxing officials, as "a Runyonesque character who enjoyed being the centre of attention." Benny had a passion for greyhound racing and local legend has it that he was banned from some of the greyhound race-tracks he used to frequent. He was involved in the boxing game for more than 30 years and managed well-known boxers such as Joe Erskine, Phil Edwards, David 'Darkie' Hughes and Lennie 'The Lion' Williams.

All the boxers he managed spoke well of him and it has been said that he was a great supporter of good causes. *South Wales Echo* boxing correspondent Dave Phillips described him as "the number one character in British boxing" while another boxing correspondent Ron Oliver wrote: "I rate Benny Jacobs as one of the shrewdest and most humane managers in the game today. He will not allow his boxers to take unnecessary punishment, and their welfare is always uppermost in

---

mind." Mickey Duff, another legend in the boxing world, said: "Benny Jacobs was one of the wittiest men I ever met and in my opinion the best manager to come out of Wales in my time."

As well as being a shrewd businessman, Benny, it was claimed, could speak a number of languages including Italian, French, Chinese and Arabic. Not bad going for someone born in the Cardiff Docks area. It has to be said that at no time was his name linked in the press with that of Gomer Charles as a co-conspirator. However, all I know is that my late friend Reg Condon, who incidentally introduced me to Benny Jacobs at his Ringside Club in Custom House Street, Cardiff, back in the 1960s, revealed to me that Benny had asked him to place a large bet on the horse for him and that Benny had also asked some of his other close friends to do the same. Benny died aged just 69, on October 30 1981, taking his 'secret' to the grave.

1.4   THE SPARE WHEEL – BONEY M CASE

Alan Jenkins, of Church Village, Pontypridd, enjoyed a six-year riding career as a jockey at flapping tracks across south Wales, including Pontyclun, Glynneath, Tondu, Glasbury, Fforest Fach, Castleton, Monmouth, PenyBont and Llandridnod.

He recalled a three-runner six furlong race at a meeting in Fforest Fach in 1956. The bookmakers had made a horse called Sylvia the favourite at 5-4, Ginger Boy was a 6-4 shot and Blue Boy was on offer at 10-1. All three owners got together to fix the race so that the outsider of three would win. They gave the riders their instructions and put their money down. But the bookies smelled a rat and as the horses were going down to the start they were shouting and screaming "No race! No race!" but all to no avail.

The starter sent the horses on their way and Blue Boy soon went five lengths clear down the back straight with the other two runners racing alongside each other in no hurry at all, but at the same time trying to make it look as though they were riding for all they were worth. However, going round the final bend, Blue Boy stumbled and his rider Alan Jenkins fell off! The result being that Sylvia, the favourite, went on to win by a neck from Ginger Boy. It's not very often bookies cheer the favourite home but on this occasion they did. And as Alan says "There is no such thing as a certainty in racing."

Back in the 1980s, a story of mine appeared in *The Sporting Life* about Gwyn Griffiths, a South Wales racehorse owner and green-grocer of Heoly-Grug, Gilfach Goch, who in 1984 was banned from attending or sending horses to any official race meetings for 15 years.

He was found at a Jockey Club hearing to have deliberately misled his horse's trainer and race course stewards. His horse Spare Wheel won the Mildenhall Claiming Stakes at Newmarket in the August of that year, supposedly running for the first time in nearly two years. It was backed from 20-1 to 12-1 before the race.

But Jockey Club officials, acting on anonymous information, discovered Spare Wheel had been running at unofficial 'flapping' meetings in South Wales under another name, Boney M, and had won at an unlicensed meeting at Llysworney, near Cowbridge, earlier in the summer.

The three-year old mare was disqualified from the Newmarket race it won by two-and-a-half lengths and Mr Griffiths was banned from attending any premises licensed by the Jockey Club for 15 years. The Jockey Club hearing found that top Newbury trainer Mr Peter Cundell, who had leased the horse from Mr Griffiths, was unaware that it had been running in flapping races in the Vale of Glamorgan.

Mr Griffiths told me at the time that he thought the ban was excessive. "Others who had been involved in doping racehorses and bribing jockeys had been let off more lightly." He said the reason for the size of the penalty was the Jockey Club's attitude to flapping meetings, which they consider illegal and are outside their control. "The question I want to ask the Jockey Club is why they look down their noses at flapping meetings. They recognise point-to-points which are similar. I think it's just a matter of snobbery", he said.

A Jockey Club spokesman explained that any horse which had previously run at an unlicensed meeting was automatically banned under Jockey Club rules from being entered for an official race. Mr Griffiths had broken this rule in addition to having misled Mr Cundell and the Newmarket stewards. "As far as the rules of racing are concerned, flapping is illegal", said the Jockey Club spokesman. Flapping at that time was widespread in Wales, and the previous time anyone had been hauled up by the Jockey Club for sending a horse to a flapping meeting was more than a year previously and on that occasion the offending owner was banned for just one year.

On July 7 1986 I revealed in *The Sporting Life* that: "Owner Gwyn Griffiths who was banned from attending or sending horses to any meeting run under Jockey Club rules for 15 years, won the richest race ever held at a Welsh unlicensed meeting at the Ely Valley Racing

Club races at Llysworney, near Cowbridge on Saturday. Griffiths, a green-grocer from Mid-Glamorgan, won the £1,000 first prize when his eight-year-old gelding Alpha got home by a neck from Little Saint."

1.5   UP THE SPOUT

Jeff Thomas in 2011

Up The Spout, who was qualified with the Glamorgan Hunt, with young Jeff Thomas in the saddle lost his maiden tag when landing a 16-runner maiden race at the Monmouthshire Hunt point-to-point at Raglan Castle in 1951. Jeff's father, Mr Herbert Thomas, had bought the horse which had come from Newmarket after the war for £120 from a Mr Packer who ran a riding school in Bridgend.

Not the best of jumpers, Up the Spout went on to win two more point-to-points that year, the adjacent at the Tredegar Farmers and the members' race at the Glamorgan. As Jeff weighed only seven stone, Up the Spout had to carry six stone of dead weight in the latter race.

The following season, Up the Spout looked like trotting up in a point-to-point at Belmont only to fall and sadly break his neck. But far from being a maiden, Up The Spout was in reality another horse, John French which had run under Jockey Club rules on the flat and who, three years before with Jeff aboard, then just 13, had won the £160 Welsh St Leger in the Vale of Neath!

A young Jeff Thomas on Up The Spout

Up The Spout and Jeff Thomas in action

1.6 MASTER FREDERICK WAS A RINGER

The Carmarthen Open Steeplechase dated to 1850 and was the principal race on the first day of the Carmarthenshire Steeplechases.

Jack Rees, of Llanboidy, we are informed in Tom Rees's *Racing Reminscences*, was "a noted flat and steeplechase rider, and huntsman of the Maesgwynne pack of hounds." Born in 1819, he rode in the colours of Mr Bowen Davies, Maesycrugiau, and proved his capabilities at Carmarthen on the old racecourse and at other meetings now long gone.

On the death of Mr Bowen Davies, he transferred his services to Mr W R H Powell and it was on Mr Powell's six-year-old Hazard that he won the race three times – 1850,1851 and 1853. William Archer won the race in 1854 on Petworth and Jack Rees who rode St David the following year, was awarded the race after Mr William Jones's Master Frederick, which was placed first, was disqualified for "fraudulent entry."

It was proved that Master Frederick was in fact a horse known as Lottery, which had won several steeplechases in Ireland. Mr Jones, a Carmarthenshire solicitor, would not accept the ruling of the racing authorities so the case was tried at Carmarthen Assizes. It was a long drawn out affair and several important racing officials, including Admiral Rous, "the greatest racing authority of his time," and numerous witnesses from Ireland were called.

Mr Jones had claimed that he had bought the horse believing that it was a maiden – a horse which had never won a race – and was completely exonerated from participation with fraudulent intent. But the costs incurred at the lengthy hearing, which went against him were reported to have been "very heavy."

Early race meetings in West Wales were held over banking courses. Jack Phelps is seen here taking a bank at the Carmarthenshire point-to-point in 1948.

2

THE GAMBLING COUPS

2.1 AM I BLUE'S ASTOUNDING WIN

The first thing to be said about the Am I Blue story is that the British Horseracing Authority (BHA), more than 12 months after the race, completely cleared Am I Blue's owner/trainer Delyth Thomas of any wrong doing whatsoever and that they would be taking no action. What they did say though, was that the case had spawned fresh integrity concerns which the BHA were looking into but wouldn't say who was involved.

Mrs Thomas pointed out to me that her explanation for the improvement in the filly's form was accepted from the start. She told me that Am I Blue's vast improvement was down to a change in race riding tactics and also that Am I Blue had a number of spinal therapy sessions leading up to the race. In fact, she told me that it was Bridgend's Annabel Thomas, no relation I understand, who had worked the miracle on her filly.

Mrs Thomas told me that much was made by the media of Am I Blue's Hereford win but little was said in the press when she was cleared of any wrong doing. Am I Blue's controversial Hereford win was not her last win at the track. She has since won a number of races when the racecourse has staged Arabian horse racing fixtures. When Am I Blue romped home a 19 lengths unchallenged winner of the obscure Wyvern Ices Handicap Hurdle at Hereford Races on September 1 2010, 'all hell broke loose' as they say. As one racing reporter put it: "There was outrage in some quarters, amusement in others."

The four-year-old filly, owned and trained by Delyth Thomas at Aberkenfig near Bridgend, had been backed from 25-1 to 5-1, despite having woeful form. In her three previous races she had been beaten out of sight by 22 lengths, 75 lengths and 88 lengths when finishing in last place. To make matters worse, her intended jockey, Cowbridge's Dean Coleman, a former leading Welsh point-to-point rider and now a 5lb.claimer, was replaced by Richard Johnson a top jockey who is one of only two riders – the other being the legendary Tony McCoy – to have ridden more than 2,000 winners.

The proud owenr/trainer Delyth Thomas and jockey Peter Carberry with Am I Blue after it had won the Design Mares' Handicap Hurdle at Ffos Las on April 25 2011.

When the stewards asked Thomas if she had an explanation for her filly's dramatic improvement in form, she told them that it had had spinal therapy and had benefited by a change in race-riding tactics in as much as she was allowed to dictate the pace rather than being held up.

Mrs Thomas told me that in the immediate aftermath of the race: "I was in a state of shock having seen my horse win so easily and was expecting at best for her to run into a place." The stewards, however, noted her explanation and stipendiary steward, Simon Cowley, told the *Racing Post* "There was nothing suspicious to investigate." Very strange indeed seeing as that Am I Blue had been heavily backed not only on the racecourse but in betting shops earlier that morning.

As for the change of jockey, there were several conflicting explanations for the switch. One was that Coleman's car had a puncture on the way to the races, another that he was not feeling well and had a dental appointment while Mrs Thomas told me: "There was nothing sinister in the jockey change. The truth of the matter is that Dean has been going through a period of disillusionment with racing as many jockeys do from time to time." She also said that his grandmother had been ill and he had been up most of the night and was not feeling well. Be that as it may, Dean was spotted leaning over the rails in the winner's enclosure.

As for the gamble on the horse, which is reported to have cost bookmakers half-a-million pounds, Mrs Thomas told me: "I have no idea who backed it. All I had on her was a tenner each way on the Tote. I know nothing at all about betting anyway."

The national press made much of the fact that prior to Am I Blue's astounding win, Mrs Thomas had trained just two winners, with the same horse, Timidjar, who won for her five years previously at 14-1 and 11-1. But, as it happens, she was no stranger to saddling winners as she was well-known in the world of Arabian horse racing as a leading owner/trainer and a few weeks earlier her Jamaahir had won the Emirates Airline Premier Handicap

Dean Coleman

Stakes and was just one of more than 100 winners she had trained in the 15 years or so that she had been involved in the sport.

Am I Blue was a former inmate of Tim Vaughan's Aberthin yard in the Vale of the Glamorgan when she was then owned by Cardiff bookmaker David Lovell who, as we know, (see the Dead Or Alive story) likes nothing more than an old fashioned gamble. Tim, who failed to win with the filly in five or six starts, went on record as saying that despite the filly's recent poor form she had been placed for him on a few occasions and that a case could have been made out for her as she was running for the first time over a distance that really suited her. But as for rumours that Am I Blue had been given a pre-race trial at Tim's place this was denied by Mrs Thomas who said: "I trained her on my own circular gallop and she has not being tried out anywhere else."

Five days after her controversial Hereford win, Am I Blue romped home a 22 lengths winner at Newton Abbot, again ridden by Richard Johnson but this time going off at 5-6 odds-on favourite.

Although the Hereford stewards did not hold an inquiry into the race, Paul Struthers, head of communications for the British Horseracing Authority later announced: "When a horse wins showing improved form, having been heavily supported and subject to a jockey change, it is vital for the integrity of the sport that all of the facts are established. It remains entirely possible that everything was above board, but we will be looking into all of the circumstances of Am I Blue's victory at Hereford."

2.2   THE OYSTER MAID AFFAIR

In Wales before the Second World War there were race fixtures galore at places such as Cardiff (Ely Racecourse), Newport (Caerleon Racecourse), Cowbridge, Pembroke and Tenby. And had it not been for the great gambling coup that was engineered at Tenby in 1927, it is possible that some of those meetings would still be operating today.

No-one seems to know, or more accurately, no-one wants to say, who financed the infamous coup. Famous National Hunt jockey, turned thriller writer, Dick Francis, who was born near Tenby, said that the coup was "probably the biggest and most bitterly resented betting coup National Hunt racing had ever known". Although I am aware of several versions of the Tenby Oyster Maid scandal, one person who was actually at Tenby that cold, windswept, snowy January afternoon revealed to me – some years ago now – "that a certain Tenby publican made between £60,000 and £70,000 as a

A rare picture of Oyster Maid

result of backing the horse", which by any standards was a lot of money in those days.

Skulduggery in horse racing often occurs in low selling races and this was the case when eight runners faced the starter for the Licensed Victuallers Selling Handicap Hurdle over two miles with prize money of £50. Three of those runners – Oyster Maid, Bubbly and Fairy Light – were trained by local trainer David Harrison, who has been described as "a big square shouldered fellow with a gruff voice."

Oyster Maid, a four-year-old mare, was owned by Ben Warner, and was returned at starting price odds of 100-6 (16-1). But, it was said that the best odds available on the course were 8-1. This was not really surprising seeing as that all of the jockeys who were involved in the coup, just like the starting price reporter, had been promised the starting price odds to £50!

All the money on the track was going on Mr Harrison's third runner, the 12-year-old Bubbly owned by Ben Warner's close friend Ted Arnold, the well-known cricketer. Bubbly, a 2-5 odds-on favourite, was ridden by the legendary Welsh jockey Fred 'Dick' Rees who has been described in the saddle as "incomparable and the greatest National Hunt jockey of all time." Oyster Maid was partnered by Billy Stott, later to become a champion rider

George Lort Stokes on his Pembroke Lad

23

himself. Fairy Light was ridden by Mr Harrison's right-hand man Tommy Duggan.

Snow and rain lashed down over the course as the runners lined up making it almost impossible to see what was happening, but once the horses went out of view at the far end of the course the jockeys in on the act are understood to have impeded those who weren't and then slowed to a walk allowing Oyster Maid and Bubbly to 'fight out' the finish where, at the last hurdle, Oyster Maid drew away to score by five lengths.

The race was hardly over when all hell broke loose. Some bookies had taken hefty bets on Oyster Maid. Several of them refused to pay out and others simply did a runner. However, it was the starting price bookmakers that took the real hammering as hundreds of telegrams for Oyster Maid had arrived at betting offices country wide just a few minutes before the start of the race. Street corner bookies were also clobbered, their locked timing bags all revealing bets large and small for Oyster Maid. The full extent of the damage was soon to become apparent and the *Western Mail* reported: "In writing yesterday with reference to the last day's happenings at Tenby, I ventured surprise at the victory of Oyster Maid over stable companion Bubbly. A big starting price coup had been engineered and it transpires that several bookmakers in a large way of business will have cause to remember that Oyster Maid won when settling their accounts."

I was told that the nearest telephone the bookmakers could use at Tenby was a gentlemen's mansion called Bryn Hir which stood on a hill overlooking the course about half-a-mile away. They had an arrangement with the owner of Bryn Hir to place a tic-tac man there whose job it was to signal to the course any large bets that were placed with the starting price operators. On an ordinary sort of day the tic-tac man would have been able to signal the course so that the bookies could hedge their liabilities by shortening the odds about Oyster Maid. But with the visibility that day down to zero due to the snowstorm the tic-tac man had an impossible task. The snowstorm, it seems, was fortuitous and did not form part of the plan.

However, this really was the end of Tenby races as few bookies or racegoers bothered to attend there ever again. Many of the off-course bookmakers even refused to take bets on horses running at the track. Over the next few years the crowds dwindled and those racegoers who did attend had to put up with small fields and short odds. It has been suggested that the gambling coup was organised to help race secretary George Lort Stokes, town clerk of Tenby, a former amateur rider of note who had fallen on hard times. Between 1906 and 1922, Lort Stokes won many of the point-to-points that were held over the haphazard banking courses in West Wales. In 1906 over the Tivyside banking course, situated between Cardigan and Newcastle Emlyn, he won the open race on his Cambrian completing the course within 12 minutes. At the Seymour Allen hunt races, held at Cresselly in 1909, he landed the United Hunt Cup on Topthorne after falling and remounting. The following year when the meeting was held near Flemington Farm, Tenby, he rode a hat-trick with Sloe Gin, Hopping Tom and Corina. A popular winner of his was Cardigan's Joy on whom he won at the South Hereford and Ross Harriers meetings. Perhaps his best horse was Pembroke Lad, on whom in 1909, he won at the Pembrokeshire Hunt, Weston–super-Mare Hunt and the Maesprior Steeplechase at Carmarthen Steeplechases.

The sad thing is that the Oyster Maid affair signalled not only the end of Tenby races and Lort Stokes, who was said to have committed suicide, but also the demise of Welsh horse racing in general.

2.3 THE WELSH WINNER OF THE EPSOM DERBY

In the long and illustrious history of the Derby, only one Welsh horse has ever won. It was George Frederick, which triumphed in 1874. George Frederick was owned and bred by William Sheward Cartwright, a solicitor, colliery owner and Lord of the Manor at Llandaff in Cardiff. Mr Cartwright named his racehorses after members of the Royal family and districts in and around Cardiff where he had a long business and residential association.

THE RACECOURSE, EPSOM DOWNS.

Epsom Racecourse home of the Derby

In his *Riding Recollections and Turf Stories*, the famed jockey Henry Custance, who rode George Frederick, had this to say: "Eccentric in manner, he (Cartwright) was always in good heart...My first success in the scarlet jacket and black cap – Cartwright's racing colours – was on Fairwater, named after his own place in Wales, in the Great Northampton Stakes of 1863". Another horse Mr Cartwright owned was a steeplechaser called Penarth and in Custance's view the best horse he ever rode for Mr Cartwright was Ely, or The Beautiful Ely, who won among other races the Ascot Gold Cup and the Goodwood Gold Cup. But it was Mr Cartwright's George Frederick, named after the second son of the Prince of Wales, which made racing history by becoming the only horse bred in Wales to win the world's most famous flat race.

Bred at Ely Farm in Cardiff, George Frederick was said to be a big, gross, heavy shouldered chestnut, out of a mare called Princess of Wales whom Mr Cartwright had repeatedly put to the stallion Marsyas. Trained at Wroughton, near Swindon, by Tom Leader, it cannot be a coincidence that there is a Wroughton Place and a Cartwright Lane in the Ely/Fairwater district of Cardiff. The once-hamlets of Ely and Fairwater are now populous suburbs of Cardiff and are divided by the main London to Swansea railway line.

Mr Cartwright backed George Frederick to win thousands of pounds after the horse had done a scintillating trial run, and so confident was he of winning the Blue Riband of the Turf that on the morning of the race he wrote 30 telegrams to friends informing them that it had won! In a field of 20 runners, George Frederick won in a canter, at odds of 9-1, two lengths from Lord Roseberry's Couronne De Fer. Some racing historians claim that George Frederick won a substandard Derby. Yet he won very easily in a time just a fraction slower than the immortal Ormonde clocked when winning in 1886.

There were great rejoicings in Wales where church bells were rung and bunting strung up in the streets. Brass bands paraded the streets and when the news reached Newport, where Mr Cartwright also had business and residence associations, his racing colours were hoisted from the town hall. *The Monmouthshire Merlin* told its readers that: "Mr Cartwright was congratulated by the Prince of Wales after the race" and *Punch* magazine printed a poem under the heading George Frederick's Feat.

This feat of thine, O wonderous horse
What other horse could do?
The Derby win on Epsom Course,
And pull a Cartright through!"

After the Derby, George Frederick had a training mishap and was eventually retired to stud. He became difficult to handle and several of his grooms sustained broken limbs on entering his stable. However, he sired a long list of horses of which perhaps the best was Frontin, winner of the French Derby.

George Frederick

Local legend has it that George Frederick was buried under an oak tree outside a public house in Fairwater, Cardiff. It is true that some years ago a skeleton of a horse was found by building workers in the area but it is my belief that the skeleton was of George Frederick's stable companion, Volturno, who had acted as his pacemaker in the Derby. My research revealed that George Frederick was shipped to America where he went blind but retained full possession of his powers. In 1893 he was moved to Canada and three years later died there at the age of 25.

As for Mr Cartwright he later gave up all connections with the Sport of Kings and went to live at Stow Hill in Newport where he died of a brain haemorrhage on May 2 1890 at the age of 69.

2.4 WHEN PERCY'S BETTING COUP BASHED THE BOOKIES

That great racing character Percy Woodland assured himself of a place in Grand National history when riding Drumcree to victory in the 1903 race followed by a further triumph in 1913 with Covertcoat.

Born in 1884, Woodland rode his first winner in a steeplechase at Lingfield Park at the tender age of 13. He was said to have been equally as good on the flat as he was over-the-sticks and having ridden two French Derby winners (Maintenon in 1906 and Or Du Rhin in 1910) few would disagree. Much admired for his dry humour and his somewhat dapper appearance, Woodland endeared himself to all who met him. There was, however, one occasion when he wasn't very popular with the Welsh bookmakers, and

Bookmaker Danny Davies with professional sprinter Eddie Williams

that was the day he landed a huge gamble at Cardiff's Ely Racecourse on the occasion of the 1929 Welsh Grand National.

As sharp as the proverbial razor, Woodland, when he was riding and training in France before the First World War, had been called before the stewards of the National Hunt Committee to explain the discrepancy in the form shown by his ride, Wild Aster at the Hurst Park and Nottingham meetings that January. He had crossed the Channel with this horse to land a number of nice little touches at small country meetings throughout England. The stewards were not entirely satisfied with his explanation and informed him that his actions were open to the gravest suspicions. But as there was no conclusive evidence he got away with a caution.

After the war, Woodland, who had also won the Grand Steeplechase at Auteuil on two occasions, returned to England and it was from his big Cholderton yard in Wiltshire that he landed one of the biggest gambles of his extraordinary racing career. It was certainly the biggest gambling coup in the history of Wales's most important horse race.

The Welsh Grand National, now run at Chepstow, was first held at Cardiff's Ely Racecourse in 1895 when it was won by Tom Cannon's Deerstalker. Of the many Welsh tracks the one at Cardiff was the most important, attracting the best horses like Cloister, Father O'Flynn, Golden Miller and Brown Jack to name just a few. Run over three-and-a-half miles, and worth £785 to the winner,

Danny Davies (left) with Jim Wilde and Mr Wilde

A packed Ely Racecourse

a then record number of 21 horses faced the starter for the 1929 race. These included 18-year-old Willie Payne's mount Great Span, who would probably have won the Aintree Grand National the previous year but for his saddle slipping at the penultimate fence when travelling like a winner.

Other runners that caught the eye in the parade ring that day were Skrun Prince, ridden by Billy Stott and Welsh jockey Dudley Williams's mount Harewood, but before long all eyes were on a clipped trace high seven-year-old grey gelding called Monduco, owned by a Mr A Bendon, who had a long scruffy tail and carried not one ounce of superfluous flesh on him.

This son of Isard 11, who was having his debut run in Britain, was being

Over The Sticks at Cardiff's Ely Racecourse, 1927

The totalisator and grandstand at Ely Racecourse.

backed for pounds, shillings and pence. Two of the racetrack's best known bookmakers Jimmy Jones and Danny Davies had chalked up odds of 20-1 on their boards for a horse which, apparently, had little form to recommend it at all. From 20-1 down to 12-1 and then 8-1 there were so many takers for Monduco that he eventually went to post a 2-1 favourite. And in the race itself the French-bred Monduco, ridden with great gusto by Irishman Jack Moloney, who had earlier that year ridden the great Easter Hero to finish second in the Aintree Grand National, got home by a length from Ruddyman, partnered by Eric Brown, with Beech Martin, ridden by the amateur Mr Rayson, a further length away in third place.

The late Albert Davies of Cardiff, son of Danny Davies, who took over his father's bookmaking business, told me some years ago that Monduco took many thousands of pounds out of the ring that Easter Tuesday. No-one will ever know how much, but it was a considerable sum. "There were a few empty bookmakers satchels that day I can tell you," recalled Albert. And he added: "Of course we learned later that Monduco was formerly a horse known as Le Mont du Coq, who was no mean performer in France." Percy Woodland had laid out Monduco for this race and once again he had made fools of the Jockey Club stewards and in doing so he had taken a number of Welsh bookies to the cleaners. Jack Moloney was destined to

Captain Pat Brain's Blue Pencil, which won many races at Ely Racecourse in the 1930s.

finish runner-up on another two occasions in the Aintree Grand National so at least winning the Welsh equivalent was some small consolation. As for Percy Woodland he went on to train a great number of winners and ended his racing days, unbelievably as an official Jockey Club starter!

2.5   THE GAMBLE THAT FAILED

A report in the *Racing Post* in July 2009 told how a horse trained by Alan Jones at Coedkernew, between Newport and Cardiff, pulled off "a real old fashioned gamble."

Secret Dancer, partnered by leading Welsh jockey Christian Williams, which had been pulled up in his only two other races over hurdles, romped home by nine lengths from the hot favourite High Gales ridden by champion jockey Tony McCoy.

Backed from 40-1 on the betting exchanges, the former inmate of James Fanshaw's Flat racing yard, ended up a 9-2 chance. Jones told the press that the owner John Spence, who paid 50,000 guineas for the horse, was a gambler who liked to back his horses and after Jones telling him that the horse was running well this is what he did.

But not all the 'real old fashioned gambles' come off and one that didn't was the one I reported upon some 30 years ago. In the April of 1979, I revealed in the *Western Mail* that former leading National Hunt jockey Barry Brogan had fallen on hard times and was working as a stable hand in a small South Wales permit holder's yard.

County Meath-born Brogan had been the legendary trainer, Fulke Walwyn's, first stable jockey. He had left Ireland in 1966 to become first jockey in Ken Oliver's Hawick stable and during his riding career had many major successes. On one occasion he rode five winners during an afternoon's racing at Wolverhampton and some thought him unlucky not to have won the 1975 Grand National when the horse he was riding, Hi Ken, came down when leading at the 21st fence.

But with the success came the heartbreaks. The highly strung Brogan beset by weight and drinking problems found that owners and trainers were no longer requiring his services. Found guilty of offences under the Rules of Racing when he failed to fulfil three riding engagements at Haydock Park in 1976, Brogan's path was a downward one from that moment on. I reported then that Brogan was living in the hope that the Jockey Club would one day renew his licence and that in the meantime he was mucking out the stables of permit holder John Williams in the Welsh village of Dinas Powis.

But the former brilliant horseman, who had early in his career been assistant trainer to another legendary figure, Tom Dreaper of Arkle and Flyingbolt fame, and who had briefly held a trainers' licence on the death of his father, Jimmy Brogan, was doing a lot more than mucking out. He had in fact been brought over from Ireland by South Wales businessman Peter Murphy, who had met Brogan when on a greyhound buying trip, to train a horse with the purpose of bringing off a huge gambling coup.

Murphy and Williams were supported by another racing enthusiast Alan Davies, and all three were partners in a book at various racing meetings and point-to-points. Mount Shasta, the horse Brogan bought for them, was said to have set them back between £5,000 and £7,000. Brogan, who was living with Murphy at the time, put his knowledge of training horses to good use slowly bringing the little horse to its peak form. John Williams may have been the trainer in name but it was Brogan who rode the horse in all his gallops as well as feeding and grooming it. He also dealt with the entries and drove it to the racecourse.

To see how good Mount Shasta really was Williams got hold of another horse called Splendid Again who had won three hurdles races when trained by Jenny Pitman and who at one time had been owned by Peter Murphy.

A trial gallop told them all they needed to know and the race selected to land their coup was the Crediton Opportunity Selling Handicap Hurdle at Devon and Exeter on the Whit Monday of 1979, which was just one of a number of race meetings that took place that day.

In his previous four starts, Mount Shasta had been completely unfancied and had never been shorter than 33-1, while the best position he had managed to obtain was a ninth place at Towcester. On the morning of the race, teams of money handlers set off early for the Midlands with bundles of money which was to be placed , in small amounts not to attract attention, and as late as possible to make sure the money could not get back to the track. However, when the betting opened up on the racecourse, Mount Shasta was only on offer at 4-1 which was a ridiculous short price for a horse with little or no form to speak about. Clearly, money had gotten back to the racecourse and in fact a representative for one of the largest betting shop syndicates, Coral Bookmakers, later admitted to having taken a lot of money for the horse and sending it back to the racecourse in an effort, a successful one at that, to reduce the starting price on Mount Shasta. Bookmaker William Hill later reported big bets for the horse in its London and Birmingham offices.

In the race itself, which was run in a torrential downpour, Mount Shasta's Jockey, 21-year old claimer Ken Dorsett, had his mount travelling well throughout and was travelling like a winner when six flights from home a bridle pin snapped causing Mount Shasta to run out. After the race, the local stewards interviewed Dorsett and Williams and recorded their explanation that the pin had snapped in the bridle.

As for the amount of money that was placed on Mount Shasta, some reports put it as high as £20,000 enough anyway for the racecourse security services and the Jockey Club to launch an enquiry. Williams and Davies claimed to have put on "only £800 between us" but there were rumours that bets as large as £500 had been placed on the horse. No one will ever know the true amount of money that was wagered on Mount Shasta but rumour had it that, had the little horse won, Davies, Williams and Murphy would have been £200,000 richer.

As for Barry Brogan he told *The Sporting Life*'s Brian Radford: "I never had a shilling on the horse. It was my job to train and place it. And it was never blatantly stopped. I bought the horse and I worked hard on it. I loved the little horse. He was absolutely right on the day, but the bridle snapped and ruined everything. It's the first time a bridle has snapped with me in all my career. The horse was pulling hard and that can only be the explanation."

2.6 DEAD OR ALIVE

Dead Or Alive, a six-year-old bay gelding owned by Cardiff bookmaker David Lovell, and trained in the Vale of Glamorgan by Abbi Vaughan, wife of trainer Tim Vaughan, landed one of the biggest betting coups seen at a point-to-point in years when winning a division of the maiden race at the Flint & Denbigh meeting at Bangor-on-Dee in March 2009.

Backed from 7-1 to 4-6 and off the boards, Dead Or Alive, partnered by Cowbridge's Dean 'Deano' Coleman, who later that season joined the paid ranks, won unchallenged by a distance. Had I been a betting man I could have in on the act as 24 hours earlier I had asked David's brother James, at the Brecon & Talybont meeting at Llanfrynach, why Dead Or Alive had been entered at Bangor-on-Dee when there were other point-to-points much closer to home. He was quite open about it and told me: "No-one will know us there and we are going to have a punt on him" adding, "He's a racing certainty."

As it happened, Dead Or Alive was one of my six horses to follow in the *Racing Post Weekender* tipping competition and months earlier this is what I had written about

Abbi Vaughan trainer of Dead Or Alive

Dean Coleman riding Dead Or Alive

Tim Vaughan

the horse. "Bought by the trainer's husband Tim at the August Doncaster Sales for £14,000, out of Michael Hourigan's yard. Ran 16 times in Ireland without success, but was staying on when finishing four-and-a-half lengths behind Concrete and Clay in a maiden at Thurles in January over two miles. Subsequently ran over three miles and likely to be suited by that trip in points".

One thing is certain, the Lovells won more than they had paid for this horse that eventually went on to win under Rules.

Bookmaker George Moir writing in John Beasley's *Big Green Annual* had this to say about the Dead Or Alive gamble. "The bigger punters tend to know where they will be accommodated and I always try to look after my regulars – though I am wary when a stranger steps up with a wad. In 2008 at Bangor I had spotted Dead Or Alive, owned by a shrewd gambler and trained by Tim Vaughan, entered in the Maiden race. I kept the price low and the horse was backed 10-1 down to odds on and won by a distance. Connections did not appear until the bigger odds had gone. Wives and girlfriends were the early punters. Vaughan then appeared despite having a winner at Warwick that afternoon. I lost £800 on the race mainly to other bookmakers at much lower odds than had been laid."

2.7   HESPERUS JUSTIFIES GAMBLE

All eyes were on Wales's most famous point-to-pointer Mandryka when he chalked-up his 30th success at the Glamorgan Hunt point-to-point Steeplechases at St Hilary in 1976. But it was a nine-year-old bay gelding called Hesperus, owned and trained by Mr M G 'Gwyn' Williams, which caused something of a sensation later in the evening when landing a massive gamble from 16-1 to 2-1 in the maiden race.

Ridden by leading rider John Beavis, who had earlier won the adjacent hunt's race on his own April Delight, Hesperous won in a canter and came home an unchallenged winner by ten lengths from Little Wyke. However, it was soon discovered that Hesperous should not have even been in the line up as he had broken Jockey Club rules by being sharpened up in three hurdle races under Rules in the point-to-pointers close season. The latest run just a few weeks earlier in a handicap hurdle at Hereford where he had finished a respectable ninth of 18 starters.

Mr Williams later attended a top-level Jockey Club inquiry and was fined £250. Hesperous was disqualified and the race awarded to Little Wyke.

2.8 MARGAM ABBEY

When racegoers saw a five-year-old grey gelding from Wales called Margam Abbey, who had never run before, being backed down from 10-1 to 5-2 in division four of the open maiden race at the Silverton point-to-point steeplechases at Black Forest Lodge on January 20 2008, they decided to get in on the act.

And they had nothing to worry about as Margam Abbey, owned, bred and trained by David Brace, and confidently ridden by Lucy Pearce-Rowsell galloped home a 20 lengths winner from the well fancied Arvakur, partnered by leading rider Polly Gundry.

David Brace, who always backs his horses when he fancies them, told me after the race: "Lucy held him up for as long as possible and he scored convincingly. I've already had several good offers for him but turned them all down".

He admitted having "a good flutter" on the galloping grey and, of course, when the punters saw him putting his money down such is his renown that they joined in too causing the odds on Margam Abbey to tumble. Margam Abbey's race might have been the last on a nine-race card, but for those who had backed him it was well worth the wait.

Lucy Pearce-Rowsell, now Lucy James

2.9 WILFRED'S WOMBLE

Cardiff bookmaker Wilfred Sherman was something of a legend in horse racing circles and at Newmarket, the spiritual home of English flat racing, there is a street named after him.

A founding father of the charity now known as Racing Welfare, he also bought the land Wilfred Sherman House now stands on. Wilfred, who stood just 4ft. 11ins., had been a former champion amateur boxer and was a

Taffy Salaman

successful member of the British team which beat the Americans on their own ground in 1935.

In 2010, shortly before his 99th birthday, I received a phone call from him. He was residing at Cordorba in Spain at the time and, still as bright as a button, he told me that he had been born in Tudor Street in the Riverside area of Cardiff and that at the age of 11 he ran errands for a local street bookmaker by the name of Billy Barron and that little did he think then that one day he would become Wales's biggest bookmaker.

He told me about the horses he owned and these included the 1968 Cheltenham Festival Triumph Hurdle winner England's Glory and Princely Son which won the 1974 Haydock Park Sprint carrying a hefty 9st.10lb.

However, when I asked him about a horse he had owned called Womble he had little to say. Womble, a winner of a maiden hurdle race in Ireland in May 1975, was trained by Taffy Salaman at Court Farm in Crickhowell. But when he left there in the January of 1977, after falling out with John Bowles, and to train at Lambourn, Womble went with him and was sold to Wilfred with the intention of landing a gamble.

Wilfred was in Australia at the time but, according to Salaman in David Ashforth's *Ringers & Rascals*, he had left instructions for him to phone a Mr Green at Ladbrokes as he would know how much to put on the horse for him. Unfortunately, Mr Green was not there, but his secretary told him that Wilfred's usual bet was £40 each way. Salaman, to be on the safe side, asked her to make it £100 each way and so sure was he that the horse, which

Wilfred Sherman

hadn't seen a racecourse for sometime, would win, he wagered £400 on Womble himself. Backed from 25-1 to 14-1, and ridden by Mark Floyd, Womble duly won the Knight, Frank & Rutley Opportunity Hurdle at Hereford. But Wilfred was not a happy man to say the least. He claimed that he didn't even know the horse was running and that he would have had £1,000 on it if he had been informed. Wilfred and Salaman fell out soon after and, as far as I know, they never spoke to each other again.

Wilfred died aged 99 in March 2010. He was responsible for getting a clause into the Safety at Work Act that required all riders working for licensed trainers to wear an improved safety helmet. This came about when on a visit to a Newmarket leading trainer he asked: "Why are apprentices, fresh out of school allowed on a horse's back without a hard hat on? The trainer just shrugged and told him: "It encourages them not to fall off." Wilfred said: "It took me some time to get that passed but my persistence paid off in the end after I had a meeting with the Home Secretary."

There's no doubt that many riders owe their life to Wilfred. He had counted among his friends many famous people such as Danny Kaye, Bing Crosby, Tommy Farr, and the Marx Brothers. On one occasion at the Savoy in London he stopped Frank Sinatra from beating up bullfighter Mario Gabri in a row over Hollywood film star Ava Gardner.

Wilfred also instigated and promoted the annual Stable Lad's boxing tournament in London which over the years has raised many thousands of pounds for charity. Best then that he be remembered for all these things rather than a row over a successful gambling coup.

2.10 TEGUCIGALPA

Bridgend business man David Brace has owned and trained many winners over the years, be they between-the-flags or under Rules, but I doubt if any of them were as good as the French-bred Tegucigalpa – a race commentator's nightmare – which landed a gamble for him in the Pontispool Equine Sports Centre Hunter Chase at Taunton on February 28 2008.

Partnered by Lucy Pearce-Rowsell, now Lucy James, and carrying Mr Brace's black and red racing colours for the first – and as it happened only time – the seven-year-old bay gelding came home in astounding style leading throughout and winning by some 16 lengths from the more fancied Raregem after being backed from 25-1 to 12-1.

David Brace is well known for backing his horses when he fancies them and it was probably his money that caused the satchel men to reduce the odds on his runaway winner. However, had punters looked up the French form on Tegucigalpa they would have discovered that it was a winner of five races in the French Provinces, three times at Toulouse, and one apiece at Mont-De-Marsan and Avignon.

As for Lucy, 12 months earlier she had been so badly injured after a crashing fall that it was feared she would never ride again. But she had buckets full of courage and determination and had come bouncing back to

Lucy Pearce-Rowsell winning on Tegucigalpa

partner one of the best horses she had ever sat on. However, she would never ride Tegucigalpa again as it sadly met with a training accident and had to be put down.

Tegucigalpa-named after the capital of Honduras, which is also called Teguz, was declared to run, but on inspection the record of vaccinations in the passport was found not to comply with the requirements of the Rules of Racing; the stewards fined Mr Brace £130.

2.11 EVAN'S TRAINING TIPS PAID OFF

Small – time one-horse permit holders like Llancarfan's Jane Mathias are the backbone of National Hunt racing and it is always pleasing when they saddle a winner or two. Even more so when they manage to back their horse and retrieve some of their training costs. And this was the case when in August 2008 Jane, a former point-to-point rider, and a qualified accountant who worked in Cardiff, took a day off to see her 11-year old Lesdream run in a claiming hurdle race at Stratford.

Lesdream which had finished third in its previous race after a 12 month lay off, had been bought out of National Hunt trainer Jimmy Frost's yard. But now, trained by an unknown permit holder, who had never saddled a winner under Rules, the bookmakers gave it little chance and odds of 20-1 were at first freely available. Jane and her friends who had accompanied her to the races then 'went to town' backing the horse for pounds, shillings and pence as they say until the odds tumbled to 8-1.

The going was on the heavy side but Lesdream was something of a mud-lover and the little horse, brilliantly handled by Irishman Donal Fahy, soon battled his way to the front to romp home a seven lengths winner from the strongly fancied favourite Critical Stage.

Trainer Evan Williams

Jane Mathias and Lesdream

What the bookmakers didn't realise was that Jane was a neighbour of leading Welsh trainer Evan Williams who had been giving her some advice on how to train the horse. Jane said: "Lesdream was such a straightforward and happy horse. He owes us nothing and now lives out his days in happy retirement."

> Jane had made hunt-racing history in 2003 when training her mother Sue's, Sohapara, winner of the first ever £1,000 point-to-point race at the Melton Hunt Club meeting at Garthorpe.

2.12 NEARLY NOBLE LANDS A 'MONSTER GAMBLE'

What was described by the *Hunter Chasers & Point-To-Pointers Annual* as a 'monster gamble' came off at the Ystrad Taf Fechan Hunt Steeplechases at Ystradowen in the Vale of Glamorgan on May 4 2002.

The big betting coup came off in the first division of the open maiden race when Nearly Noble, a nine-year-old bay gelding, owned and trained by Robert Rowsell, and ridden by his then wife Lucy, bolted home, an official four lengths, eye-witnesses claim it was more like six, from Good Morning, ridden by James Tudor, with the favourite Carl's Boy, partnered by Ian Johnson, a further four lengths away in third spot.

Nearly Noble's form figures on the racecard read 047-0 – hardly the kind of form which would have inspired punters to have backed him. But be that as it may, someone knew something and Nearly Noble, a tall and unfurnished individual, was backed from 16-1 to 4-1 and off the board in places.

Lucy, a Welsh champion point-to-point rider, had given the horse a super ride having him in a handy position throughout and, despite a mistake at the second last fence, won easily enough. Interviewing her then husband Robert, who like Lucy had been a leading point-to-point rider himself, after the race he told me that he had bought the horse in Ireland just a matter of weeks earlier from Jim Draper son of the legendary Irish trainer Tom Dreaper of Arkle and Flyingbolt fame. Not only that, the race Nearly Noble had just won was a maiden race which is for horses that have never won a race before.

However, unknown to most of the thousands of racegoers who were at Ystradowen that day, Nearly Noble had been a virtual 'winner' when he had faced the starter. For he had actually finished first in an Irish point-to-point, a couple of seasons earlier, only to be controversially disqualified after being misdirected by a fence steward!

Nearly Noble was later sold out of Wales and the following season won three more point-to-point races.

Earlier in the day, the bookmakers at Ystradowen had faced another big pay out when another former Irish horse Power 'N' Glory backed from 4-1 to 2-1, trained by Bridgend's John Moore and ridden by Tim Vaughan, won the confined race for Irishman Cyril Campwell.

2.13 BERT'S BETS DEFIED THE ODDS

An unemployed 51-year old Cardiff chef, Humberto 'Bert' Andrade, defied the odds when he placed two different 25p each-way Super Yankee* bets in two different betting shops in September 1986. All of his ten selections won but he picked up just £4,756 for his £28.60 stake (two Super Yankees plus tax).

The winners he backed with the late legendary bookmaker John Lovell were: Days Like These (11-4); Pause For Applause (4-1); On To Glory (6-1); Scottish Green (11-2); and Ishkara (11-2).

After being given an advance of a £1,000 on his £3,256 winning bet, he showed Mr Lovell, who owned the City Road betting shop, a betting slip for another 25p each-way Super Yankee which he had placed with a rival betting shop firm, Kingsport Racing.

Mr Lovell was flabbergasted when he saw that all the five horses on it were winners: Northern Gunner (evens); Softly Spoken (5-1); Paul's Secret (6-4); Roumeli (9-1); and Duffer's Dancer (4-1).

'Bert' had won a further £1,500. Mr Lovell's son Richard, who at the time was employed by John Lovell Racing, said: "I worked it out that had Mr Andrade placed a £1 win accumulator on all ten horses it would have come to over £8,000,000." As for 'Bert', happy with his winnings, he went off to book a holiday to Madeira where he had been born.

2.14 GAMBLE WAS NULL AND VOID

At Cardiff's Ely Racecourse on March 22 1905, Messrs Gus Hogan and Campbell Russell, both well-known members of the racing fraternity,

---

* A Super Yankee bet consists of five selections in 10 doubles, 10 trebles, five four horse accumulators and one five horse accumulator. The bet is also known as a Canadian.

thought they had a good thing for the Ely Selling Handicap Hurdle with the well-bred Tiara, a six-year-old mare by Stonefield out of Delightful Lady. Owned by Mr B Ebsworth and trained by Tom Rees of Llanstephen, Tiara, who was ridden by Mr Rees's son, T P Rees, had shown good form when finishing a close second to the useful Booty at Tenby on its previous start.

So when the bookmakers chalked-up 3-1 against their fancy, between them, Hogan and Russell, lumped on £650, quite a lot of money back then. Favourite at 5-2 was Ingratitude, ridden by the famed Welsh jockey Ivor Anthony, who later would train the immortal Brown Jack.

After making most of the early running, Ingratitude faded and Jovial King, partnered by Mr Deer, and who had been in a handy position throughout, went on to win comfortably having little difficulty in shaking off Tiara and scoring by an official three lengths.

However, rumours soon circulated the course of an objection and it seemed pretty certain that of the eight flights of hurdles only seven of them had been jumped. It has been said that it was Ivor Anthony who had informed Mr Harries, the owner of the beaten favourite, that he was sure he had jumped only seven hurdles. Jockey Club rules stated that in a race of two miles, six had to be negotiated in the first mile and one more in each subsequent quarter of a mile.

In the following day's *Western Mail*, at the end of a report of the Ely races, in small print an announcement read:

'ELY SELLING RACE VOID. An objection having been laid against the winner of the Ely Selling Hurdle on Tuesday, the acting stewards Lord Tredegar, Mr W H Jenkins and Colonel Morgan Lindsay, sitting on behalf of Colonel F C Morgan declared the race null and void.'

Hogan and Russell had gambled £650 and to all intents and purposes had lost. But with the race being declared null and void all monies wagered on the race had to be returned to the punters.

It was at Newport's Caerleon Racecourse in 1924 that an objection to Simon's Glory, winner of the Tredegar Handicap Hurdle, was probably unique in the history of the turf. The objection was that instead of covering the stipulated distance of two-and-a-half miles the horses completed the two-and three quarter miles course. After much deliberation the stewards declared the race void and fined the clerk of the course £25!

2.15 PEBBLE RIDGE'S SENSATIONAL WELSH NATIONAL WIN

An eight-year-old brown gelding called Pebble Ridge, owned by Lord Glanely, trained by Ivor Anthony and ridden by Dudley Williams, hit the bookies for six when winning the 1933 Welsh Grand National at Cardiff's Ely Racecourse.

Harry Llewellyn, later Sir Harry, of Foxhunter fame, who finished fourth in the race on his own horse Silver Grail, recalling the race many years later said: "I remember the race caused quite a sensation as Pebble Ridge had finished last in all his previous races, yet he was backed down to 6-4 favourite."

There were only nine starters and Pebble Ridge, confidently ridden by Williams who had earlier won the Aintree Grand National on Kellsboro' Jack, romped home an easy three lengths winner from 7-1 chance Holmes.

Williams, who had been successful in the same race on Boomlet three years earlier, was one of a select band of Welshmen who had dominated the National Hunt scene between the wars. It was said of him that no other jockey had ever ridden the Aintree racecourse with greater skill or courage.

As for Lord Glanely he was affectionately known to the racing public as 'Old Guts and Gaiters'. He was a leading owner on the flat and he saw his famous racing colours carried to success in all the classics winning the: 2000 Guineas (Columbo – 1934); 1000 Guineas (Dancing Time – 1941); Derby (Grand Parade – 1919); Oaks (Rose of England – 1930); and St Leger (Singapore – 1930 and Chumleigh – 1937).

Born William Tatem in North Devon, he became a junior clerk with a firm of tugboat owners in Cardiff Docks and later, branching out on his own soon became a millionaire. However, he was accused of double-crossing his employees and business associates back in 1919 when he told them to back his horse Dominion for the Derby. Unfortunately, for them, he won the race with his other runner 33-1 chance Grand Parade!

2.16 THE KATESVILLE COUP

A memorable gambling coup was landed at the Axe Vale Harriers Point-To-Point Steeplechases on April 12 1989. Katesville, owned and trained by Crickhowell's Lee Bowles, and having his first race of the season, stormed home under Tim Jones, of Rudry, near Caerphilly, an eight lengths winner of the men's open race leaving his 13 rivals trailing in her wake.

Katesville at the Langeinor Point-to-Point on April 28 1990

It was reported that between £10,000 and £12,000 was taken out of the bookmakers' satchels and one bookie was said to have laid a bet of £7,000 to £300 about the eight-year-old gelding. All kind of rumours floated around the course after the race owing to the vastly improved form of the winner and the 1990 *Hunter Chasers & Point-to-Point Annual* had this to say about Katesville:

"Landed a punt of astronomical proportions from 25-1 to sixes at Stafford Cross and ran up a four-timer with equally convincing performances which included a dead-heat over four miles. Can quicken on firm and holding, but may be best if sparingly raced and kept fresh. Worth trying in a Hunter Chase. Blood-typing subsequent to the Axe Vale coup (no doubt to prove the horse was who it purported to be – warned off dad John Bowles, who once won a ringer at Newton Abbot, was fined a further £1,000 in 1989 for continuing to attend Welsh Points) proved his sire could not be Crozier as given in the Stud Book. The horse was disbarred from running until his GSB registration had been amended, but the connections ignored the ban, and Katesville was therefore disqualified from his Tredegar victory. Presumably his registration was in order before his final appearance."

2.17 THE MAN WHO TAUGHT NORTON'S COIN TO JUMP

When former Welsh point-to-pointer Norton's Coin, who scored one of the biggest shocks in National Hunt racing history when winning the 1990 Cheltenham Gold Cup at 100-1, was found dead in a field at the Carmarthen farm of his owner/trainer, Sirrell Griffiths', racing scribes rushed to their phones to get comments from his Gold Cup winning rider Graham McCourt. They also, of course, sought the comments of Sirrell and a host of other leading lights in the racing world including Jenny Pitman who trained the runner-up Toby Tobias.

However, none of them bothered to phone the man who rode Norton's Coin to his first success in a point-to-point and to his first win under rules in a hunter chase and, more importantly, who taught the horse to jump fences when schooling him over an old tree trunk long before he had won National Hunt's racing's greatest prize.

That man was Welshman Tim Jones, who won a division of the Maiden race at the Ystrad Hunt point-to-point at Llantwit Major in 1986 on Norton's Coin. Tim, who also won a hunter chase at Chepstow on the horse in 1988, was asked by former National Hunt champion jockey Peter Scudamore, guest speaker at the West Wales point-to-point dinner dance that year, which of the horses he was riding he thought would one day go on to better things. Tim told him Norton's Coin, who he said would one day win a Gold Cup.

When Norton's Coin returned to the unsaddling enclosure after his famous win, Peter Scudamore went straight over to Tim and told him: "When you told me that this horse would win a Gold Cup I thought you had had too much to drink!"

Tim said: "My sister Pip also won on Norton's Coin in a point-to-point at Erw Lon but he was a much better horse running on a left-handed track and he had never won on a right-handed one. Tim added: "At the time, I was riding Lislary Lad, the best horse in Wales, so I knew that Norton's Coin was something special." Tim has never received the credit due to him for his part in the Norton's Coin story.

His sister Pip was Wales's most famous female rider. In 1998 she became the first Welsh woman rider to win the national ladies point-to-point championship. She would have no doubt won the title on several other occasions, but for being sidelined owing to injury.

Tim Jones

Despite all the broken bones and punctured lungs – she was once on a life support machine – after being injured in a crashing fall at Nottingham – she always came bouncing back with a renowned determination. She rode her first winner, it was her first ride, at the Llangibby point-to-point in 1986 when she was just 16-years-old. She won the Welsh Ladies' title a dozen times or more and some of the good horses she was associated with were Final Pride, Gunner Boon, Matsix, Final Abbey, Kerry Solder Blue and, of course, Norton's Coin.

Leading amateur rider Pip Jones

3
THE SCANDALS

3.1 POINT-TO-POINT'S MOST CONTROVERSIAL RACE

Not many point-to-point stories made the front page of the now sadly long defunct *The Sporting Life*. One that did, though, was the one I reported on for the paper in 1993. It was the men's open race at the Gelligaer Farmers' fixture at Llantarnam, near Newport, where a large crowd had assembled to see a horse I had dubbed 'The Desert Orchid of Wales' – the Peter Bowen-trained prolific grey gelding Brunico.

Brunico, who had been a class horse on the flat and over hurdles, was almost unbeatable between-the-flags. This little horse, with his regular English rider Ron Trellogen in the saddle, was greeted with a tremendous ovation when eventually emerging the winner. But Pontypridd's Robert Rowsell, riding Alf Mahaba, and Rudry's Tim Jones on Zephyr Nights, were greeted with boos and catcalls after finishing second and third respectively in the sensational three-horse race.

When the race started, Rowsell and Jones made little attempt to make a race of it, knowing that the quirky Brunico had to be held up for a late run. Brunico finding himself in front, at first refused to jump the second fence, but when he did, and caught up with the other two horses, they slowed down again. Brunico led at the seventh, only to refuse again, as did the other two horses, and when all three managed to negotiate the obstacle, they continued at a pace which could only be described as little more than a hack canter.

It was only at the 18th of the 20 fences that Brunico took over the lead from Alf Mahaba and with Trellogen continually looking over his shoulder, Brunico eventually came to the last fence ahead of Alf Mahaba, and although strongly challenged, Treloggen and Brunico

Peter Bowen in 1993

The grey Brunico scores a sensational win at Llantarnam

teasingly kept a length in front all the way to the winning post. The winning time was surely one of the slowest ever recorded for a three-mile point-to-point, nine minutes and thirty six seconds.

When Brunico returned to the winner's enclosure, he received the loudest cheers I have ever heard at a point-to-point. However, when the other two riders reached the unsaddling enclosure, they were greeted with boos and catcalls and the crowd had been so incensed during the race that they called for the stewards to declare the farce a no-race. All three jockeys were reported to the Jockey Club, however, they in their wisdom, decided that: "the running and riding of Alf Mahaba and Zephyr Nights did not warrant the holding of an inquiry either under the regulation relating to horses running on their merits, or the rule relating to the proper conduct and good reputation of racing."

The incident marred a great day's racing for Brunico's trainer as he saddled three other winners – Duke Of Impney, Parkbride and Kyme Warrior. The three riders all received letters informing them that the stewards of the Jockey Club, having heard the evidence and viewed a video of the race, were of the opinion that there was insufficient evidence under the regulations for the matter to be referred to the disciplinary committee. And Jones, who had always claimed that he had broken no rules, told me: "I am happy it's now all over."

> Brunico ended his days in a sad way. He was reported to have sustained such severe injuries to the head and forelegs when grazing in a field that he had to be put down, a terrible end to the winner of The Daily Telegraph Trophy in 1992, who had chalked up 12 consecutive wins. He won a further 11 races in 1993 as well as the classic Dudley Cup in 1992 and 1993, being the first horse in 20 years to make a successful defence of this classic race.

3.2 SOME MAIDEN!

Having reported on the Welsh point-to-point for over half a century, I have witnessed some strange races. Take the maiden race at the Pentyrch evening meeting at St Hilary, near Cowbridge, in 1975.

Henry Blake and Prince Haven 11 jump into the lead

Dillwyn Thomas's homebred Prince Haven 11 was judged to have dead-heated with Mr A Taylor's Swedish-bred Quip. But many racegoers, including myself, were of the opinion that Prince Haven 11, partnered by Henry Blake, a best selling author of books on communicating with horses, had won the race outright. And so did the bookmakers who started to pay out over him.

However, it is only fair to point out that the winning post at St Hilary was a long way from the natural grandstand from where the races were viewed. But more fuel was added to the fire when someone pointed out that far from being a maiden (a horse who has yet to win a race) Quip had won, among other races, the Danish St Leger as well as six other races on the flat in Scandanavia!

In his previous races Quip, an eight-year-old chesnut gelding, had started at odds of 33-1 or more but on this occasion he had been well backed with several bookmakers at odds of around just 6-1 or 7-1. Most unusual seeing as he had failed to finish in his three previous starts, twice being pulled-up when tailed off, and once running off the racecourse.

Amazingly, Weatherbys in their far-sighted vision ruled that those wins in Scandanavia did not render Quip ineligible for maiden events explaining that a winner of a flat race, or a National Hunt flat race, was permitted to run as a 'maiden' in a point-to-point steeplechase.

The late Henry Blake was a modern day Dr Dolittle. His three books – *Talking With Horses, Thinking With Horses* and *Horse Sense* were best sellers at home and abroad. Affectionately known in hunt racing circles as The Major he and his family moved from Somerset to Wales in 1961. He was sadly confined to a wheelchair after a riding accident.

3.3   RIDER'S ELIGIBILITY

Point-to-point racing is an amateur sport. But in 1993, a story of mine appeared in the *Racing Post* claiming that the Jockey Club were investigating the eligibility of Caerphilly rider Tony Griffiths after discovering that he had held a professional licence for some ten years and had partnered 30 winners during the 1980s.

Griffiths, who was then working as a bricklayer, had ridden his first point-to-point 'winner' in his second season between-the-flags at the Glamorgan Point-To-Point Steeplechases at St Hilary when he had got the American-bred seven-year-old Philipponnat, owned by Mrs Annwyn Jones, home by half-a-length from Origami, ridden by Jon Parry Keen, in the restricted open race. However, as I said in my report at the time, Jockey Club rules state that only people who have held a licence for less than 30 months were eligible to return to the unpaid ranks. As the *Hunter Chasers & Point-to-Point Annual* commented, "What a ridiculous situation."

3.4 ROUGH JUSTICE

Gwynne Anthony, a younger brother of the famous Anthony trio – Jack, Ivor and Owen, had a club foot which made him very self-conscious. It was said of him that he was a wonderful horseman and he certainly rode more point-to-point winners than any of his three renowned brothers.

In one particular race he was crossed at a bank by William Campbell Davies-Evans who had recently returned to Wales from New Zealand where he had ridden in steeplechases and hurdle races with some degree of success. Born in 1873, he had commenced hunting at the age of six and was later educated at Harrow. He was a rather large, red-faced, pompous man and Gwynne vowed he would get his revenge on him. And this he certainly did by jumping off his horse on to the back of Davies-Evans and, dragging him out of the saddle, proceeded to give him a real going over.

Of course the cunning Gwynne waited until they were racing out in the country and out of sight of the crowd.

3.5 PEERLESS JIM TO THE RESCUE

One person who knew all about the racecourse gangs of the 1920s and 1930s was *South Wales Echo* reporter Bert Allen who at Monmouth Races one year had to have police protection from the notorious racecourse gang known as The Forty Thieves who had wanted him to reduce the starting price odds about one of the winners.

Bert recalled: "I was once saved from a racecourse gang of toughs by that great maestro Jim Driscoll, 'Peerless Jim' to the rest of the world."

Bert, who also reported on the boxing scene, went on: "At that time it was part of my duty as a correspondent for leading sporting newspapers to compile official betting returns at race meetings. This afternoon saw me among the milling crowds on Ely Racecourse, now a vast housing estate. Amid that colourful scene, long lost to Cardiff, of gaiety

South Wales Echo journalist Bert Allen

Peerless Jim Driscoll

and optimistic tipsters offering their fancies and hoarse bookmakers crying the odds to race-goers eager to do business with them, I strolled from the paddock across the course to the Tattersalls ring. The holiday mood seemed enjoyable. But as I passed the grandstand half a dozen rough-looking customers surrounded me and demanded to know why the starting price of the Welsh Champion Hurdle winner on the previous day was only 4-1 and not 7-1. 'That's my price and I'm sticking to it,' I said, whereupon the obvious leader of the thugs called me a string of names not on my birth certificate and threatened due consequences if I did not publish a correction. I refused to be intimidated and put on as bold a face as I could, though felt far from happy.

With that Jim Driscoll came along and leading me to the bar with an invitation for a drink asked the cause of my trouble. When I told him he said: 'Did they offer you a pony?' – £25 in racing parlance – I replied: 'No, only a thick ear' and Jim ruefully felt his own cauliflower ear and grinned.'

Not many people know that Peerless Jim Driscoll was also a bookmaker who had pitches at many race meetings and other sporting events such as the professional Welsh Powderhall Handicap foot race held at Taff Vale Park between 1903-1934. Jim, who would never have contemplated throwing a fight, had no qualms at all about asking one of the sprinters he sponsored to throw a race!

3.6 RACECOURSE GANG HANGING CAUSED A STORM

No verdict in British legal history, it was said, had created such unrest as the one that sentenced Cardiff's Danny Driscoll to be hanged in Cardiff Prison in 1928.

Daniel Driscoll and two other members of the notorious race-gang known as The Forty Thieves were sentenced to die for the murder of ex-boxer David Lewis who had tried to muscle in on their protection racket. Lewis, married with five children, had fallen on hard times and was scraping a living hiring out stools to bookmakers at local racecourses. And it seemed that some members of the gang had seen him as some sort of threat for this was at a time when protection gangs ruled the racecourses.

Bookmakers had to pay gangs for the chalk, water, buckets, sponges and lists of runners whether they wanted them or not. Those that didn't comply would find that their betting boards and stands would be turned over and smashed up or even worse.

On the first day of the two-day Monmouth Steeplechase meeting on September 28 1927, Lewis was 'invited' by Edward and John Rowlands to pay for their protection. He declined, but knowing that they would be out to get him instead of going home that night, he stayed in a hotel. The next day when the Rowlands brothers saw Lewis hiring out stools at the races they decided he should be given 'a frightener'. That night Lewis decided to have a drink in the Blue Anchor in St Mary Street and who should be in there as well but Danny Driscoll and Edward Rowlands, with John Rowlands and another member of the gang, William Joseph Price, waiting in a cafe just across the road.

Lewis left the pub, John Rowlands left the cafe and seconds later the unfortunate Lewis received terrible slashes to his throat which left him in a pool of blood on the cobble stones. One of the 'ladies of the night' tried to stem the flow of blood with cloth torn from her petticoat and Lewis was rushed to the Cardiff Royal Infirmary. The police kept a vigil at Lewis' bedside and throughout the night there were regular phone calls from the same number enquiring about Lewis' condition.

Those calls were traced to the Colonial Club a well known dive in Custom House Street and it was there that the Rowlands brothers, John Hughes, Danny Driscoll and William Joseph Price

Danny Driscoll

David Lewis

were arrested. The suspects were taken to Lewis' bedside and he told the police that he didn't know how he got his wounds and to Danny Driscoll he said: "You had nothing to do with it. We were talking and laughing together...my dear old pal".

During the trial, police had told how they found blood on 'Tich' Rowlands's clothing. But the evidence against Driscoll, who had told a pack of lies and half-truths out of fear more than anything else, was not so strong. Some people believed it significant that at three identification parades not one eyewitness, apart from two police officers whose evidence didn't tally anyway, was able to identify Driscoll.

Within hours of the verdict more than £600 was collected to help Driscoll pay the cost of his appeal, but there was no sympathy for the Rowland brothers, who have been described as

Danny Driscoll's relatives enter Cardiff Prison

St Mary Street where David Lewis was found with his throat slashed

'vicious villains'. At a jam-packed Cory Hall in Station Terrace, hundreds of Driscoll sympathisers were told that John Rowlands had maintained that he alone had killed Lewis. Sackfuls of appeal forms were sent to the Home Office and even two members of the jury, who had found Driscoll and Rowlands guilty, went to London to visit the Home Secretary to plead for the lives of Driscoll and Rowlands.

As for Driscoll himself, he wrote from Cardiff Prison: "I say I am an innocent man. The evidence against me was so slender that no jury could reasonably find me guilty, but for the fact that their minds were inflamed against me by untrue statements." On the morning of the hanging, 5,000 men, women and children stood outside Cardiff Prison singing hymns. Driscoll we are told walked proudly to the gallows, looked up to the heavens and said: "Well, they've given us a nice day for it," and added: "which noose is mine?" Meanwhile Edward Rowlands, who had to be helped from his cell, was almost unconscious. John Rowlands was to escape the hangman's noose after being certified insane while William Joseph Price was acquitted.

Cardiff's Gareth Thomas, who has studied the case in great detail for a film script he is working on, writes: "In his late teens, Dai Lewis was a successful welter-weight boxer who fought at boxing tournaments across the country. Like Driscoll he returned home from the 1914-18 war a hero, but found it hard adjusting back into ordinary working class society. Driscoll and Lewis were well known at local horse racing meetings such as Cardiff and Monmouth. They earned a living as small-time bookmakers and other schemes like the hiring out of stools to the racecourse bookmakers.

It is thought that Lewis attempted to take Driscoll's territory at Monmouth. Others believe that Lewis had tried to cheat Driscoll out of his winnings. Whatever the real reason, a frustrated Driscoll was said to have held a razor to Lewis' throat which resulted in a fatal laceration. Many believe it was an unintentional murder and that Driscoll had only intended to give him a warning. Lewis upheld the underworld code on his death bed by not saying who it was that slashed his throat. And now we will never know the truth as to what happened on St Mary Street that awful night."

3.7 PLUNGER WAS NOT QUALIFIED

Hereford's John Bryan came in for plenty of praise when he set a new seasonal race riding record when booting home his 30th winner on Little Fleur in the men's open race at the Llangeinor Hunt Point-To-Point Steeplechases on May 13 1978.

Another rider who also came in for plenty of cheers that day was Barton Williams, a colourful character, who somehow managed to force his tail-switching Plunger first past the post by just a length from the favourite Lord Belvedere partnered by Welsh champion rider Mike Williams.

Plunger, however, was not qualified with one of the required adjacent hunts and was later disqualified. It was also claimed that as a three-year-old Plunger had won a mile-and-a-half race on the flat! And the rules for the race stated that "a maiden is a horse which, at the time of starting, has never won a steeplechase, hurdle race or any other race under the rules of any recognised turf authority, point-to-point races included."

The race was awarded to Lord Belvedere, owned by Mrs June Jones, of Rudry, who said: "I have received the prize money, but it would have been nice to have heard officially from Weatherbys."

3.8   THE FORTY THIEVES

The late, great, local historian Bill Barrett told this story about a loud-mouthed member of the Cardiff Canton Liberal Club who, when the conversation turned to some of the scams and tricks practised by the notorious Forty Thieves gang, declared: "Well, I'm going to Ely Races for the Whit Monday meeting and they had better not try anything with me."

It was a sunny day on the Whit Monday but as the individual concerned walked into the racecourse he was asked for a light by a small, shabbily-dressed man. As he felt in his pocket for some matches, a few toughs closed around him and bundled him under the grandstand. Five minutes later, he staggered out unhurt, but had been picked clean of every penny and his braces had been cut. He then had the embarrassment of shuffling home across the city, holding up his trousers, with not even a penny to ride on the tramcar from Victoria Park.

When he finally got home his wife was not at all sympathetic. "In future", she scolded, "keep your big mouth closed as the gang's ears are everywhere".

3.9   UNDER ORDERS-TO LOSE!

I had the pleasure of contributing to Chris Pitt's *A Long Time Gone*, published in 1996, and which is said to be one of the best 100 horse racing books of all time. This truly fascinating book tells the story of Britain's vanished racecouses and I was honoured to be asked to provide Chris with information on the long gone Welsh race meetings such as Cardiff's Ely Racecourse and Newport's Caerleon Racecourse.

Although Chris kindly credits me with having provided him with much of the material on the Welsh racecourses, one story in which I have no claims on at all concerned Keith Piggott, father of the legendary Lester Piggott and Wales' biggest bookmaker of the time Jimmy Jones of Newport.

As well as being a bookmaker, Jimmy was also a racehorse owner and one of his horses Mr Madcap, at one time the best two-mile chaser in the country, had been entered, on his orders, at the 1926 November Newport meeting. After all, it was Jimmy's home track and he wanted all his friends to see it win there. But Jimmy, who had told all his pals to back it, appears to have had second thoughts.

Let Keith Piggott himself take up the story: "I went across to ride him thinking he was a certainty. However, the owner came up to me in the paddock and told me not to win, because all his friends had backed it with him!"

"Going to the last I was lying second and running away, so I jumped nearly on top of Billy Stott on the leader and finished second beaten by a head. The stewards had me in afterwards and I told them I lost an iron at the last. One of them then said: 'I didn't see you lose an iron, Piggott'. I replied 'No, you were on the wrong side!'"

James Edward (Jimmy) Jones was well respected throughout the horse racing and greyhound racing world. When he died, it was said of him that he "had contributed in a quiet and unobtrusive fashion to many deserving causes." Friends from far and near attended his funeral at St. Woolos Cemetery in Newport and these included the Mayor of Newport Councillor W G Rudd, JP. Major Stephen Wildman, manager of Ely Racecourse, and well-known bookmakers Stan Cottle and Danny Davies along with many sporting personalities.

Keith Piggott rode around 350 winners and these included the Welsh Grand National on Vaulx, the 1939 Champion Hurdle on African Sister and the 1927 Grand Sefton on Trump Card. His biggest success as a trainer came in 1963 when he saddled Ayala to win the Grand National.

3.10 DAB OF VICK GOT BILL IN TROUBLE

Farmer Bill Howells, of Baiden Farm, Cefn Cribbwr, near Bridgend, admits to having had a nice few gambles on his point-to-pointers over the years. But he didn't know the trouble he would get into when he rubbed a spot of Vick on the nose of his wife June's eleven-year-old Jymario before the start of the ladies' open race at the Llangeinor Hunt Point-To-Point Steeplechases at St Mary Hill in 1989.

Ridden by family friend Anabel Butler, aged 21, the blinkered Jymario, who was made the 7-4 favourite, led throughout most of the race and won unchallenged by a good ten lengths. Mr Howells, who had recently been a patient at the Princess Of Wales Hospital in Bridgend, had made a pledge that the prize money won by the horse would be donated to the hospital as a thank you for the good treatment he had received. But the Jockey Cub's dope testing unit, which had made a surprise visit to the course, took a blood sample from Jymario which was to prove positive. Mr Howells said: "All that happened was that I rubbed Vick on the horse's nose to guard against infection as so many horses seemed to have had colds. It seemed a harmless practice and, after all, Vick is more or less a children's cold remedy. It had been used before but it seems a new rule came out when I was in hospital. People have found ways of introducing drugs to horses that can be concealed with the use of camphor which is basically what Vick is."

The trouble is that Vick is a banned substance and although Mr Howells was cleared of any intentional wrong doing, he was fined £100 anyway!

3.11 TROUBLE AT TIVYSIDE

Scandalous may be too strong a word to use, but the happenings at the Tivyside Hunt Point-To-Point Steeplechases at Pantyderi in April 1996 were controversial to say the least.

The trouble started after the Intermediate race in which Mister Horatio, under Mark Lewis, had finished first by a comfortable six lengths from the grey Metro Style. A steward's inquiry followed and it was found that several of the leading horses, including Mister Horatio, had gone the wrong side of a marker. However, the result was allowed to stand after it was discovered that the clerk of the course had moved one of the markers without informing anyone, least of all the riders!

Mark Lewis on Mister Horatio

Further controversy was to follow after the first division of the maiden race. Gunner Boon (number nine), ridden by Wales's most famous female rider Pip Jones, went straight into the place reserved for the winner after appearing to have got up on the line to beat Dustys Trail (number six) ridden by Robert 'Choc' Thornton, now a leading National Hunt jockey, by a neck.

Mr Brace, Gunner Boon's owner/trainer was congratulated by Peter Bowen, now Wales' leading National Hunt trainer, who trained Dustys Trail. But the judge thought otherwise and ruled that Dustys Trail had won by a head! After a very lengthy steward's inquiry in which the judge was given the chance to reverse the placings, the result remained the same and an objection which Mr Brace had made, was overruled.

It seemed to almost everyone on the racetrack, with the exception of the judge of course, that Gunner Boon had won. Some said by as much as half-a-length or so! Mr Brace, sponsor of the prestigious Dunraven Bowl Hunter Chase which is held at Chepstow, complained to the judge and officials in no uncertain manner on how the meeting had been run, and who could have blamed him?

The point-to-point 'bible' *Hunter Chasers & Point-to-Point Annual* for 1997 commented: "Gunner Boon passed the post half a length in front at Pantyderi but the blind judge got it wrong and the feeble stewards (already reeling from the shock of some misplaced markers in an earlier race) could not get him to change his mind (West Wales Pointing at its finest!).

3.12 MILTON WAS TAKEN FOR A RIDE

The much respected Milton Bradley, who has trained horses near Chepstow Racecourse for more years than he probably cares to remember, revealed to Graham Green in the *Racing Post* on June 9 2011 how he had given up any hope of recovering £160,000 he said he had lost when training for a woman who had pretended to be a multi-millionairess.

Alison Meryl Johnson, 54, was jailed for six years and nine months in her absence at Plymouth Crown Court just days before but she was rearrested after being found by police. Her victims, and there were many, said the six charges she had admitted, totalling £811,292 were "only the tip of the iceberg" and Bradley's losses were never part of the criminal proceedings. She had a number of horses with Bradley and these included Enchantment, Tapau, Billy Bathwick, Johannian, Royal Supremacy, Stars

At Midnight,Regal Flight and Tadeo. And despite selling two of them in a bid to offset the unpaid training fees and reimburse him for two of the horses she had instructed him to buy at Tattersalls, Bradley was still "around £160,000 out of pocket."

Bradley told Green: "I don't like to count it up because it really hurts, and what is more I will never get that money back because she hasn't got any,I have just had to accept it." He added: "I regret the day our paths crossed and she was the biggest woman con-artist I've ever come across."

"When we had a few winners for her, she said to the staff she must bring them a drink down, but she'd arrive here and say she'd left her purse at the service station and that she'd see them right another day. Of course that day never came. I trained quite a few winners for her, but it didn't make any difference and it's good to see she has been caught up with at last."

Johnson had made out that when she had divorced her husband Ian, she had received a settlement of around £2 million while another victim had understood that the settlement had been between £4-5 million! Several of her victims came from the Vale of Glamorgan area where she once lived. She persuaded her victims to invest large amounts of money in high yield offshore deals but never invested a single penny in any offshore accounts. She stole £327,000 from Mrs Jennifer Griffith who had known her since she was just 15-years-old through a shared interest in horses.

Mrs Lynda Williams, who had been recently widowed, said she was a trusted friend and had believed her when she had said she had received a huge divorce settlement. She lost £45,000 to Johnson and there were others including Charles Vicary £150,000, Stanley Dusting £235,000 and Lynne Callaway £50,000.

The thefts had taken place between 2001 and 2008 and the money was used to fund her lavish lifestyle which included owning racehorses, buying big houses and expensive antiques. Prosecutor Andrew Oldland told the court that Johnson had "wriggled over a number of months and years to avoid the inevitable and had avoided court for sentence." Judge Graham Cottle said to call her a confidence trickster was far too generous a description. "You befriended and targeted vulnerable people in a thoroughly cold and calculating fashion and plundered their life savings. You have left a trail of financial devastation for your victims. You painted a totally false picture of yourself and your financial situation in order to trap unsuspecting people who considered you to be a friend and part with their money in the belief you were acting honestly in their best interests. It was breathtaking dishonesty carried out on a large scale by a completely unscrupulous woman which has left lives and finances for a number of people in a state of ruin." Detective

Constable Richard Teague said: "Alison Johnson is a deluded, manipulative and thoroughly evil woman. She has shown no remorse for her crimes."

Johnson had owned 14 horses with Bradley over a five year period before she had been declared bankrupt in 2007. Presumably she must have backed these horses from time to time. Well, if that is so, one wonders how much of her victims' cash ended up in the bookmakers' satchels!

3.13 CHECK UP WAS CHECKED OUT

After a nine-year-old bay gelding called Check Up had won the men's open race at the rearranged Curre and Llangibby Hunt Point-To-Point Steeplechases at Howick, near Chepstow, on March 14 2010, I interviewed the winning jockey William Oakes and owner/trainer Andrew Leyshon in the unsaddling enclosure.

Mr Leyshon, who owned a car dealership in Bridgend in addition to training a few point-to-pointers, told me that he had bought the horse after it had won a Chepstow seller in 2007. What he obviously didn't tell me

William Oakes on Check Up

was that Check Up had twice run under the name of Patsy's Boy at Hawick in Scotland and that he had also run him on two occasions in Dingle in Ireland under the names of The Stig and then The Paparazzi.

Another of Mr Leyshon's horses, Dancing Lyra – which before joining him had won six races and some £73,000 in prize money – had also run the previous year from Mr Leyshon's yard at unrecognised 'flapping' meetings in Ireland and Scotland. On May 26 2011, the disciplinary panel of the British Horse Racing Authority found that Mr Leyshon, a registered owner had committed a breach of the Rules of Racing in respect of his training and owning Check Up and Dancing Lyra when the horses had run under different names at unrecognised meetings.

Faced with photographic evidence, Mr Leyshon made an admission that he was in breach of the Rules and Regulations and he was warned off for nine months. In addition to being warned off, Mr Leyshon was banned from attending race meetings and point-to-points and was not allowed to visit licensed premises such as training yards. Check Up and Dancing Lyra were also banned from running either under Rules or in point-to-points.

Mr Leyshon told the *Racing Post*'s Graham Green. "I obviously deeply regret what I did and I held my hands up and gave the reasons for what happened to the panel. I was shown the flapping world by an ex-business partner and he introduced me to Dingle in 2007 when we went on a family holiday, and it came from there. I have been given a nine-month ban, but I will be back fighting and stronger when it is finished."

The amiable owner/trainer Mr Leyshon, of Merthyr Mawr - one of the nicest people on the Welsh point-to-point circuit one could wish to meet and who is always willing to talk to race reporters - certainly lived up to his word by coming back stronger than ever and has saddled a number of winners since. One of the most recent being Distant Sound which was a good winner at the Gelligaer Farmers Hunt point-to-point at Lower Machen in May 2015.

4

THE FLAPPERS

4.1 ROBERT KING'S REMINISCENCES OF PONY FLAPPING

Pony racing or 'flapping', as it was often called, was prolific in Wales, particularly in the mid west and south from the 1920s and involved the racing of ponies and horses on the flat and usually on makeshift racecourses.

The phrase pony racing should not be confused with the legitimate pony race meetings that were held under the Rules of Racing and so ably documented by Leonard Janes in his book *Pony Racing*. Janes records that a recognised pony race meeting was held in the 1930s at Clyne Racecourse in Swansea. However, the earliest racecard I have seen was for a meeting of 'pony races' at Glais in the Swansea Valley dated 1924 and there are references to 'flapping' in the book *Racing Reminiscences* by Tom Rees of Llanstephan, which was published in 1923.

The salient aspect of flapping is the fact that is was not recognised by the Jockey Club and completely unlicensed, and that status has not been altered since the British Horseracing Board (BHB) took over the administration of horse racing in the United Kingdom.

As an activity, the BHB does not have a problem with pony racing and will sanction meetings provided they are managed by a constituted committee and that ponies of 14.2 h.h. and under take part. When thoroughbred horses became involved the opportunity for corruption presented itself and most flapping meetings would stage what the organisers called an 'Open Race' in which only thoroughbreds would compete. In these events, horses that were also registered to run under the rules of a recognised racing authority often took part.

This practice was not tolerated by the Jockey Club/BHB and those caught taking part at these unrecognised meetings would be warned off the turf. Owners and trainers carried the heaviest penalties and the riders, too, if they rode at flapping meetings at the same time as being registered to ride by a recognised turf authority and would be banned from holding a licence to ply their trade under rules.

It has long been accepted that pony flapping is a good grounding for young jockeys and many well known names started their careers by riding ponies. One often hears or reads in the media about how many successful Irish riders learned their trade at pony meetings.

The heyday of flapping in Wales was the period immediately following the Second World War and it ran until the mid 1970s. Since that time the sport carried on in a fragmented form at one or two locations, primarily in the Vale of Glamorgan.

Initially the sport was run in divisions separated by the height of the ponies (this altered sometime in the 1970s when the divisions merely referred to thoroughbred horses and their ability) and the handicap system used would that be of a staggered start. The races were started by the firing of a starting pistol.

Some meetings were mixed, wherein trotting races would be held but many

'Flapping' Race card from Swansea in 1950

meetings were dedicated to galloping ponies and horses. Naturally, because these meetings were unregulated, corruption was rife. Most meetings saw some stunt or other carried out and these stunts took many forms. From the basic 'stopping' horses arriving at a meeting, usually from England, who were at the same time running under the Rules of Racing. They had been brought to Wales to land a coup (they would be handicapped to run at the meeting they attended on the day they arrived) and

NOTICE TO BOOKMAKERS AND PUBLIC—On the "all right" a WHITE FLAG will be shown on the Number Board. If a Horse is "disqualified," a RED FLAG will be shown. All Bets should be paid immediately the White Flag is up.

6ᴰ **Official Race Card.** 6ᴰ

GLAIS RACES

(UNDER WELSH RACING RULES) ON

SATURDAY, JUNE 2ND, 1923.

GATES OPEN 1·30 p.m. FIRST RACE 3·0 p.m. PROMPT.

Officials—

Judge	W. LEWIS, Esq., Cwrt-y-Bettws, Neath.
Handicapper	J. PRICE, Esq., Merthyr.
Starter	D. M. EVANS, Esq., Ystalyfera.
Clerk of the Course	ESAIAH LEWIS, Esq., Glais.
Clerk of the Scales	J. SLACK, Esq., Glais.
Secretary	J. REES, Esq., Glais.

Acting Stewards under W.R.P.A.

Mr. TOMKINS, Llansamlet, and Mr. J. PREECE, Llanelly.

Stewards, Foot Events, A. JOHN, Esq., Trebanos, & W. HOWELLS, Esq., Glais

ONLY OFFICIALS ALLOWED ON THE COURSE.

The Promoters reserve the right to re-arrange the Races as they think fit.

Will Hopkin, Printer, Pontardawe.

they were not always successful as there were some pretty quick horses at these unlicensed meetings.

Sometimes a false favourite would be created by those owners and trainers 'in the know' putting money on a horse that didn't belong to them, and which didn't have much of a chance, so as to lengthen the odds on their own horse. Then when their horse went out in the betting there would be a mad scramble of a team of men hitting the line of bookies simultaneously placing their bets.

During the 1950s, '60s and '70s the sport was most active at a host of locations across southern Wales including: Tondu; Troas; Glasbury; Aberyscir; Monmouth; Swansea; Ammanford; Glyneath; Pontrhydfendigiad; Cothi Bridge; Gilwern; Llyswerney; Llansannor; Llandysul; Llanelli; Llangadog; Kingston; Haverfordwest; Tredegar; St Clears; Usk; Bridgend; and Glantawe.

One aspect of the running of open horses or thoroughbreds was that those who ran usually on flapping tracks would sometimes appear on licensed racecourses in England under different names, of course. I'm not for a moment saying that those licensed trainers or jockeys knew that their charges had a double life so to speak.

There were two instances that I became aware of and it was either in 1965 or 1966 when I was asked to ride work for a well-known businessman who lived near Mumbles. One Monday morning on Swansea beach together with

6d.   Official Programme   6d.

Bridgend Races

(UNDER WELSH RACING RULES)

Cowbridge Road Racecourse, Bridgend,

ON

Saturday, May 29th, 1926.

First Event at 4 p.m.

OFFICIALS:

Judge—Mr. H. C. HIBBERT, Bridgend.

Handicapper—(Horse and Foot), Mr. JACK PRICE, Merthyr.

Starter—Mr. A. TOWNSEND, Bridgend.

Stewards— { Mr. E. LEWIS D.C., Aberdare.
{ Mr. A. TOWNSEND, Bridgend.

Clerk of Course & Scales—Mr. GEO. JONES, Bridgend.

Secretary—21, Park Street, Bridgend.

Note—All prize money will be sent to successful competitors by Cheque within seven days of the Meeting.

All Prizes for Horse Events are subject to 2½ per cent deductions under the Welsh Racing Rules.

another flapping jockey – he rode a horse we knew as Goldie, who ran under rules as Sam Benedict, and who was trained by Captain Ryan Price. I rode a bay horse who ran at flapping tracks as Brownie and under Rules as Bounteous and trained by P. Dent in Surrey.

I did know that these two horses led a double racing life but thought nothing of it. Brownie ran at the flaps and I would sometimes ride him what happened elsewhere wasn't my concern. Anyway, Brownie worked very well and won the gallop with a stone in hand as they say. This was really good form as Sam Benedict had been a recent winner under Rules. I told my father about the double lives of these that many of the flapping horses led and he was a conscientious follower of racing in general and did like a gamble.

On the Tuesday following the gallop on Swansea beach, my father asked me to reiterate Brownie's licensed name. He knew that I had worked him the day before and said with a degree of annoyance that the owner could have said he was running him on the Monday afternoon at Alexandra Park and had won a mile handicap at odds of 33-1 ridden by Willie Carson!

That same year, at one of the early jumping meetings, Sam Benedict won a two mile hurdle race for Captain Ryan Price when ridden by Josh Gifford. I must point out that I'm not saying for a moment that Messrs Carson, Gifford, Dent or Price were aware of the double life led by these horses.

One afternoon at Tondu races I was asked to ride a horse in the open race by an owner who was unknown to me. I agreed and the connections of the horse told me the horse was called Eyes Down, a winner under Rules and for flapping purposes it went under the name of Jack or something daft like that. Many racing folk who fancied trying to land a coup on a Welsh flapping track often didn't realise one important point. The bends were very tight on some of the courses and could only be described as wide corners. If a horse couldn't naturally 'track', the jockey was in big trouble. The owners of Eyes Down assured me that the horse would cope with the bends but unfortunately he couldn't and, although running on the right leg into a bend, he went wide at every one and over a mile at Tondu there were six bends to negotiate. On the straights Eyes Down made up a lot of ground but could eventually finish no better than third behind a horse from Seven Sisters called Easily Led. The bookmakers were obviously on their guard against these ringers and Eyes Down went off the odds-on favourite after being backed from 2-1. We were beaten by three lengths but had lost at least ten lengths on the bends. Eyes Down and his friends were not seen on a Welsh flapping track ever again.

Considering the whole object of running ponies at these meetings was ultimately to land a gamble very few ponies ran throughout the season on their merits. 'He's on stop' would be a commonly heard whisper. And believe me when the instruction to the rider was not to win, that horse certainly wouldn't win. It was not difficult to appear to get beaten through lack of ability. Many races had more than 20 runners. The starts would be staggered sometimes over a distance of 80 yards but to the practised observer it wasn't too difficult to see that this pony or that one was deliberately being prevented from winning. There were so-called stewards but action against a crooked ride was rarely, if ever, imposed. The punter with no connection to a pony was gambling on the premise that the buyer should definitely beware and the day when the owners of a pony decided that "they were off", the secrecy would have befitted a military operation. A race would have been selected and when the bookmakers opened up the odds, the connections of the pony that was trying would quietly at first place money, usually with a team of punters on another fancied pony ignoring their own. Slowly the bookmakers, who always trying to guess what was going on, would lengthen the pony's odds and when they did the team would get to work.

I recall one incidence at Tondu when the instruction was "not to win, but get placed and finish fast". The idea being to appear to be trying but that the pony was not quite good enough. A pony called Jill, a reliable mare, was being primed for a race at Aberyscir in Brecon. It was a mile race with plenty of bends and there were around 18 runners who during the course of the race went out of sight on two occasions. No problem in getting lost but half of the field fell or hit a hawthorn hedge at the first bend and some ran out at the second, leaving just a handful of survivors. Up the back straight Jill was literally cantering while the remainder of the field were being pushed along. But once out of sight the brakes went on and as the ponies entered the straight Jill could be seen languishing some ten lengths behind. However, a late flourish saw her beaten by a short head after a blatantly corrupt ride.

The following Wednesday, against supposedly better class ponies, she won by five lengths at Aberyscir. Sometimes things didn't go all to plan, and again owing to dishonesty, on this occasion on the part of the owners. One set of connections would agree to 'stop' their pony and another set of owners, put into motion, rider and selected punters, that their pony was the one today. But the first set of connections would quietly back their pony and then instruct their rider to win at all costs thus trapping the second set of owners who would lose a substantial amount of money. After the race all hell would break out with the connections, who had been duped, viciously fighting with the other band of owners.

Police presence was virtually non-existent at flapping tracks so the outcome of disagreement was often resolved by fist-fights. Similar scenarios were played out every Saturday and most Wednesdays throughout south and west Wales between Easter Monday and early October and the level of corruption must be the main reason why the sport has all but disappeared. Owning and training a racing pony was a means into racing for many people that didn't involve the expensive bureaucracy of recognised racing. If the organisers of meetings had not carried into their fixtures the open races that facilitated proper thoroughbreds then it legally could have been recognised. Although such recognition wasn't that important to most owners they just loved racing and landing a well-organised gamble. In the early 1980s, a few pony meetings were held at Margam Park in Port Talbot. These were not sanctioned by the Jockey Club but they could have been if an application had been made because they were strictly for ponies under 14.2hh.

The meetings were run in the same way as those held in Weston-super-Mare, Cheltenham, Bedford and Lingfield, but with one exception. At Lingfield, the meetings were not well patronised either by the ponies or members of the public and they drifted into the realm of the local history books. I'm grateful that they did appear when they did during that decade because I owned a pony called Cennen Gambler who was a prolific winner at those meetings.

Pony racing only now exists under the auspices of the Charles Owen Point-To-Point Pony Racing Series and very entertaining they are. Already this aspect of pony racing has thrown up a very successful jockey, National Hunt's Rhys Flint, while others include David Prichard and Tom David.

4.2   A FAR FETCHED STORY

One Cardiff man who remembers the many flapping meetings that used to take place throughout Wales just after the last war is former Plaid Cymru councillor Lynne Davies who as a young lad lived in Penygroes in West Wales. Lynne used to ride in these rough and ready races and he partnered his father Uriah's game bay mare Far Fetched to success many times at racecourses such as Llanybydder, Synod Inn, Llanedy, Capel Cynnon and Fforestfach. It was at the last named meeting that Lynne won the Welsh Pony Championship over seven furlongs on Far Fetched in 1950 easily accounting for Mr D Jenkins's five-year-old Joey who carried two stone less than the aged Far Fetched.

The prolific Far Fetched, named after Rhondda boxer, Tommy Farr, competed in races for ponies under 13.2hh or under 14.2hh and was so versatile that she won races from six furlongs to a mile-and-a-half. And it was nothing unusual for Far Fetched to win two races during the same afternoon. Big money could be made betting at these long-gone meetings by running a horse down the field a few times and then, when the odds were right, having a good old fashioned gamble.

However, Lynne's father, an ostler at the local coal pit, who owned and trained Far Fetched was not a gambling man, being quite content to pick up the prize money to be won. But that did not stop Far Fetched's happy band of followers, the villagers of Penygroes, who used to lay on a special

Hugh Isaac, the young Bynea jockey

Far Fetched

Far Fetched

bus to the races, having a good flutter on their favourite horse and more often than not they had plenty to sing about on the way home from the races.

Before they handicapped the horses by weights, they handicapped them by giving them various starts just as they did with foot runners at athletics meetings. With Far Fetched usually being among the backmarkers, Lynne had to weave his way to the front so as to get a good position to make his challenge. Accidents and foul play did occur and Lynne still has the scars from when he had either by mistake or purposely found himself under the hooves of a dozen or more horses. The jockeys had to negotiate tight and twisty bends and there could be as many as five circuits or laps of the racecourse to complete. Sadly, one of Lynne's jockey pals, Aneurin Evans, was killed in a race-riding when he was just fifteen in 1949.

What racegoers didn't know was that Far Fetched was very well bred being by Saleve, a winner on the flat and over hurdles, and whose sire was Derby winner Spion Cop! The story is that Saleve was visiting a neighbouring farm on stud duty when he jumped a fence and, unbeknown to his owner, W H Craven, who kept the Lion Royal Hotel, Aberystwyth, mounted a 'Section A' Welsh mountain pony the result, of course, being the prolific Far Fetched!

Far Fetched winning at Llangadog in 1948 with Will James in the saddle

POSTSCRIPT

When Cardiff bookmaker John Lovell was tragically killed in a traffic accident just yards from his home, in April 2008, horse racing lost one of its great characters. John started a betting revolution in 1995 when he introduced a computerised betting system to Britain's racecourses. He was also the first bookie to bring the world of horse race betting into the 20th century when opening the first two-in-one betting shops with traditional betting facilites, alongside a trading room where punters sat at computers and played on betting exchanges.

I had known John, the son of a Cardiff boilermaker, for half-a-century and shortly before he died I had interviewed him for my Turf Talk column in the *Western Mail*. He told me then that the racing scene, which ironically he had played a part in changing, had lost "a lot of its buzz."

The racecourse characters he had known: The Duck; The Ferret; Joe the Rat; Simon 'Dodger' McCarthy; and Cardiff bookies Benny Jacobs, Benny Edwards; Johnnie Kenneally; Sammy Fletcher; Jimmy Thomas; Bill White; George Parsons; and Billo Griffiths had, just like the racecourse tipsters Captain Colley, Prince Monolulu and Gully Gully, all disappeared.

He said that in those days, racecourse bookmakers had to pay someone for the chalk, water, rag dusters and so on for their betting boards. But the computerised betting machines that John had introduced had put paid to all those fiddles. John, a former pupil of Cardiff's Howardian High School, owned a number of racehorses over the years and these included The Womble, Blue Snake, Mullacrew and, best known, Churchtown Boy, which, after he sold it, went on the finish runner-up to the legendary Red Rum in the 1977 Grand National.

A successful businessman, at one time John had 14 betting shops. He also had a number of greyhounds which raced at the Cardiff Arms Park, the best being a dog called Bear Cat.

He had recently returned from a horse-racing trip to Australia and Hong Kong when I interviewed him and he told me: "Our racecourses are years behind them. We could learn a lot from them." John was Chairman of the South and West Bookmakers Association and he had come to enjoy attending local point-to-point meetings more than race meetings proper. On the Saturday before he died, he approached me at the Monmouthshire Hunt Point-To-Point at Llanvapley, which I was reporting on, and he asked

John Lovell

me would I like to go with him to see his new point-to-pointer Sams Lad, at trainer Tim Vaughan's new racing yard, at Aberthin in the Vale of Glamorgan. He said:" I will phone you in the week to make arrangements to pick you up."

They were the last words he ever spoke to me. Members of John's family made the long trip to Cilwendig in West Wales to see his horse Sams Lad win the restricted race at the Llandeilo Farmers Hunt Steeplechases under Deano Coleman. There had been a minute's silence on the course before racing, in John's memory, and when his funeral took place later, hundreds of racing enthusiasts from all over the country attended to pay their respects. Had John lived he would have no doubt told me enough tales of the turf to fill another book.

To finish this book I'd like to recall the joyous day in 1990, when Llangadog's very own Norton's Coin famously won the Cheltenham Gold Cup at odds of 100-1 and thousands of Welsh punters were triumphant, with the bookies left to count their losses. There were no scandals that day, just plenty of successful gambles!

Wales's most famous racehorse, Norton's Coin, with owner/trainer Sirrel Griffiths

BIBLIOGRAPHY

History of Cardiff Racecourse (Brian Lee, Cwm Nedd Press 1980).

Welsh Steeplechase Jockeys (Brian Lee, Cwm Nedd Press 1993).

The Races Came Off - The Story of Point-To-Point Racing in South & West Wales (Brian Lee, Welsh Sporting Publications 1985).

The History of the Welsh Grand National: From Deerstalker to Supreme Glory (Brian Lee, Tempus Publishing 2003).

When Diamonds Were Trumps (Reginald Herbert, Walter Southwood, London, 1906).

Steeplechase Jockeys: The Great Ones (Tim Fitzgeorge-Parker, Pelham Books, London 1971).

Fifty Years of Racing at Chepstow (Pat Lucas, H G Walters Ltd, Tenby 1976).

Famous Gentlemen Riders At Home and Abroad (Charles Adolph Voight, Hutchinson & Co, London,1925).

The History of Steeplechasing (Michael Seth-Smith; Peter Willett; Roger Mortimer; John Lawrence:

Michael Joseph, London, 1966).

Encyclopaedia of Steeplechasing (Patricia Smyly, Robert Hale, London, 1979).

Master of Hounds (Fred Holley *et al*, V A Holley, Merthyr Tydfil, 1987)

Passports To Life (Harry Llewellyn, Hutchinson/Stanley Paul & Co. Ltd, London, 1980).

Timeform Chasers & Hurdlers (Portway Press, various editions)

Hunter Chasers & Point-To-Pointers (Weatherbys Chase, various editions).

Taken For a Ride (Brian Radford, Arthur Barker Ltd, London, 1981).

Ringers & Rascals (David Ashforth, Highdown, 2003).

A Long Time Gone (Chris Pitt, Portway Press Ltd, 1996).

The author has also drawn material from the following publications: *The Sporting Life, Cardiff & Merthyr Guardian, Cardiff Times, Western Mail, The Monmouthshire Merlin, Racing Post, South Wales Argus.*

ST DAVID'S PRESS

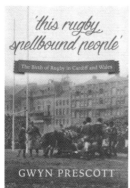

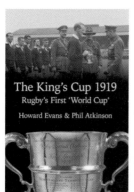

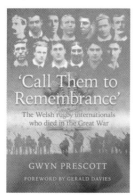

ST DAVID'S PRESS

THE BOXERS OF WALES
CARDIFF

'Some of the greatest boxers in Britain have come out of Cardiff and this book is a must read for fight fans, whether you're Welsh or not.' *Colin Hart, The Sun*

'This book is not just about the famous fighters, it's about the forgotten heroes.'
Steve Bunce, Boxing Broadcaster & Journalist

'A compelling and fascinating study.' *Claude Abrams, Editor, Boxing News*

'Boxing fans in and out of Wales will love this collection of mini biographies profiling no less than 50 classic boxers from the Cardiff area...An indispensable guide to Cardiff boxers and a great resource for compiling those pub quizzes!'
South Wales Argus

'...a long overdue reminder of how much Cardiff has given to boxing. The verdict? A knockout.' *Dan O'Neill, South Wales Echo*

978-1-902719-26-9   160pp   £14.99   PB

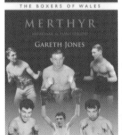

THE BOXERS OF WALES
MERTHYR
ABERDARE & PONTYPRIDD

'masterpiece... a must-read for any boxing fan...Compelling stuff.'
Steve Lillis, News of the World

'The Valleys of South Wales have produced many fighters known worldwide ... but this book reminds us that there were others who lit up the ring in their day.' *Gareth A. Davies, Daily Telegraph*

'For generations of Merthyr's youth, boxing has been as much a means of self-expression as a way out of grinding poverty. This book does full justice to a sporting tradition that has shaped the town's character and given the world some unforgettable champions.' *Mario Basini, Author, 'Real Merthyr'*

978-1-902719-29-0   160pp   £14.99   PB

THE BOXERS OF WALES
RHONDDA

'When Boxing News marked its centenary in 2009 by choosing the best British boxer of the previous 100 years, we opted for the one and only Jimmy Wilde. But the Rhondda produced many other outstanding fighters, as this book reminds us.' *Tris Dixon, Editor, Boxing News*

'When it comes to in-depth research, they don't come much better than Gareth Jones – as his latest tome perfectly illustrates, with a trawl through the Rhondda's staggering boxing history. The likes of the great Tommy Farr and Jimmy Wilde get the Jones treatment, along with a host of tales surrounding so many boxers from this mining area that produced such a rich seam of boxing greats.'
Kevin Francis, Boxing Correspondent, Daily Star

978-1-902719-33-7   160pp   £14.99   PB

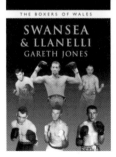

THE BOXERS OF WALES
SWANSEA & LLANELLI

'My co-commentator, Enzo Maccarinelli, keeps telling me what a great fight town Swansea is. And here's the evidence. It's not just about the big names, like Colin Jones, Ronnie James and the Curvises – here you can learn of the only Welsh-speaker ever to win a Scottish title and the Llanelli girl who took on Germany's boxing queen. A great read!'
John Rawling, Commentator, BoxNation

'Wales has a rich boxing history and there is no one better than Gareth Jones at bringing vividly to life the exploits of the many fine Welsh fighters, from the famous to the largely forgotten. This book is a must for all serious boxing fans.' *Graham Houston, Editor, Boxing Monthly*

978-1-902719-450   176pp   £14.99   PB

St David's Press

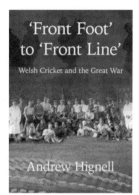

CRICKET IN WALES

'FRONT FOOT TO FRONT LINE'

WELSH CRICKET AND THE GREAT WAR

'Sport prepares you for many of the challenges you will face in life, but certainly not for war. The friendship and camaraderie of the changing room helps you to bond and unite a team and, with this in mind, I can fully understand why so many sports teams joined up en masse ... but just as these men played together on the cricket fields of Wales, many died together on the battlefields of Europe.' **Huw Morris, from his Foreword**

'Front Foot' to 'Front Line' commemorates the significant contribution made by the cricketers of Wales to the military services during the Great War of 1914-18 and follows the major themes and battles of the war to chronicle those professional and amateur cricketers from Wales who lost their lives as servicemen on the bloody battlefields of Europe as well as those who returned home permanently affected by their experiences of the horror of warfare. The book also highlights the involvement of others involved at the grassroots of Welsh club cricket who also served.

978-1-902719-42-9   224pp   £16.99   PB

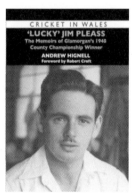

CRICKET IN WALES

'LUCKY' JIM PLEASS

THE MEMOIRS OF GLAMORGAN'S 1948 COUNTY CHAMPIONSHIP WINNER

'I can but only admire Jim's contributions during Glamorgan's Championship-winning summer of 1948 or his efforts with the bat against the 1951 South Africans at Swansea...[without him] I can only wonder at how different the course of Glamorgan's cricketing history might have been'.
Robert Croft, from his Foreword

In 2014 Jim Pleass was the longest surviving member of Glamorgan's County Championship winning team of 1948, the first time the Welsh team won the highest honour in county cricket.

Jim was a very lucky man, as the book explains his narrow escape from certain death when he stormed the Normandy beaches on D day in 1944. If it wasn't for the over-exuberance of a driver on another landing craft, Jim would never have graced the cricket field wearing the daffodil of Glamorgan County Cricket Club.

978-1-902719-36-8   128pp   £14.99   PB

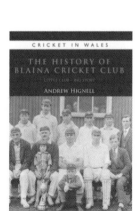

CRICKET IN WALES

THE HISTORY OF BLAINA CRICKET CLUB

LITTLE CLUB, BIG STORY

'It's a wonderful story of a club with a truly big history, and I hope you're as captivated by it as I was. It only remains for me to say that I'm sure you'll enjoy this fantastic book, and here's to the next 160 years!'
Emma Peplow, from the Introduction

Drawing on the memories, photographs and personnel recollections of those directly involved with the Blaina club from the times when coal was king, through the years of the decline in the iron and tinplate industry to the modern years of mine closure and de-industrialisation, Andrew Hignell has not only produced a cricketing history of Blaina, but also a social history of the town.

978-1-902719-32-0   192pp   £16.99   PB